EDI DEVELOPMENT STUDIES

Does Privatization Deliver?

Highlights from a World Bank Conference

Edited by

Ahmed Galal
Mary Shirley

The World Bank
Washington, D. C.

The Economic Development Institute (EDI) was established by the World Bank in 1955 to train officials concerned with development planning, policymaking, investment analysis, and project implementation in member developing countries. At present the substance of the EDI's work emphasizes macroeconomic and sectoral economic policy analysis. Through a variety of courses, seminars, and workshops, most of which are given overseas in cooperation with local institutions, the EDI seeks to sharpen analytical skills used in policy analysis and to broaden understanding of the experience of individual countries with economic development. Although the EDI's publications are designed to support its training activities, many are of interest to a much broader audience. EDI materials, including any findings, interpretations, and conclusions, are entirely those of the authors and should not be attributed in any manner to the World Bank, to its affiliated organizations, or to members of its Board of Executive Directors or the countries they represent.

Because of the informality of this series and to make the publication available with the least possible delay, the manuscript has not been edited as fully as would be the case with a more formal document, and the World Bank accepts no responsibility for errors. Some sources cited in this book may be informal documents that are not readily available.

The material in this publication is copyrighted. Requests for permission to reproduce portions of it should be sent to the Office of the Publisher at the address shown in the copyright notice above. The World Bank encourages dissemination of its work and will normally give permission promptly and, when the reproduction is for noncommercial purposes, without asking a fee. Permission to copy portions for classroom use is granted through the Copyright Clearance Center Inc., Suite 910, Rosewood Drive, Danvers, Massachusetts 01923, U. S. A.

The backlist of publications by the World Bank is shown in the annual *Index of Publications*, which is available from Distribution Unit, Office of the Publisher, The World Bank, 1818 H Street, N.W., Washington, D.C. 20433, U.S.A., or from Publications, Banque mondiale, 66, avenue d'Iéna, 75116 Paris, France.

Ahmed Galal is a senior economist and Mary Shirley is the chief of the Finance and Private Sector Development Division of the World Bank's Policy Research Department.

Library of Congress Cataloging-in-Publication Data

Does privatization deliver? : highlights from a World Bank conference
  / edited by Ahmed Galal, Mary Shirley.
       p.   cm.—(EDI development studies)
    Includes bibliographical references.
    ISBN 0-8213-2589-2
    1. Privatization—Congresses.   I. Galal, Ahmed, 1948–
  II. Shirley, Mary M., 1945–   .   III. International Bank for
  Reconstruction and Development.   IV. Series.
  HD3842.D63   1994
  338.9—dc20   93-23358
                                                     CIP

CONTENTS

PART 3. SYNTHESIS AND POLICY IMPLICATIONS

FOREWORD

This volume summarizes the presentations at a two-day World Bank conference on the welfare effects of privatization, held in Washington, D.C., on June 11–12, 1992 and attended by some one hundred senior policymakers, academicians, and advisers from around the world. Its objective was to disseminate the findings of two years of research conducted by the World Bank and Boston University analyzing twelve cases of privatization of state-owned enterprises in four countries. The detailed analysis of the case studies will be available in a forthcoming World Bank publication. Meanwhile, this volume provides a preview and an overview of the research project and shares some of the insights of the discussants at the conference. The issues discussed in this volume are an important part of EDI's program of seminars on privatization. This volume is a valuable tool both for trainers involved in classroom instruction, as well as for readers who are interested in learning more about the implications of privatization of state-owned enterprises.

Amnon Golan, Director
Economic Development Institute

ABOUT THE CONTRIBUTORS

Nancy Birdsall is executive vice president of the Inter-American Development Bank. She was formerly director of the Policy Research Department at the World Bank, where she worked on human resource development, the environment, and adjustment, fiscal, trade, and privatization issues. She was also a member of the World Bank's Research Committee. Prior to this, she served as chief of the environmental division in the Latin America Region at the Bank.

Eliana Cardoso is associate professor at the Fletcher School at Tufts University and a research associate of the National Bureau of Economic Research (NBER). She is also a member of the Joint Committee on Latin American Studies of the National Science Research Council.

Roger Douglas has served as a cabinet member in the New Zealand government. Formerly minister of finance in New Zealand, Mr. Douglas is known internationally as the driving force behind the reform of the country's economy during the period 1984-88. This reform included major deregulation of financial markets, corporatization of state trading departments and adoption of privatization policies, as well as dramatic reform of taxation systems. He has also served on the Public Expenditure and Commerce Parliamentary Select Committee and was Shadow Minister of Trade and Industry and Shadow Minister of Finance.

Ahmed Galal is a senior economist in the World Bank's Policy Research Department. He also provides policy advice on a broad range of issues concerning public enterprise, divestiture, and private sector reform in several countries in Latin America, Asia, and Africa. He has written a number of articles on public enterprise reform, institutional reforms, divestiture, and private sector development. Currently, he is working on issues of regulation of public utilities, sale of public enterprises, and the changing role of the state.

Heba Handoussa is a professor of economics at the American University in Cairo. She has been economic adviser to the Minister of Industry since 1980 and has served as the Egyptian counterpart in joint studies with the World Bank and as a member of steering committees for several other studies. She has been the principal Ministry of Industry negotiator with the World Bank on the structural adjustment program since 1986. Ms. Handoussa has published many articles and papers and is the author or coauthor of several books, among which are *Egypt: Issues of Trade Strategy and Investment Planning,* and *Labour Market Study: the Manufacturing Sector, 1970-1984.*

Leroy P. Jones is professor of economics and director of the Public Enterprises Program at Boston University. He is the author of several books and numerous articles in the field of public enterprise and government/business relations in developing countries. His overseas experience includes nine years residence in four Asian countries and work on about twenty other countries.

Johannes Linn is the World Bank's vice president for Financial Policy and Risk Management. He joined the World Bank in 1973. He is coauthor, together with Amarendra Battacharya, of a study entitled *Trade and Industrial Policy in the Developing Countries of East Asia* published by the World Bank Mr. Linn was staff director of *World Development Report 1988* which dealt principally with issues of public finance in development. Between 1988 and 1991 he served as senior economic adviser in the Development Economics Department, as the director of the International Economics Department, and as director of the Country Economics Department.

Rolf J. Lüders is professor of economics, and research program director at the Institute of Economics of the Catholic University of Chile. He has been director of the capital market development program of the Organization of American States, has served on the board of directors of private enterprises, and has been secretary of finance in Chile. He has coauthored several books and numerous journal articles. A book on *Privatization in Chile*, with D. Hachette, has just been published in Spanish and English. In addition to his academic activities, he also does occasional consulting for several organizations including the World Bank, the United Nations, and the International Center for Economic Growth.

Jorge Marshall is minister of economy in Chile. He was formerly under secretary of the ministry of economics and before that worked at the ILADES-Georgetown University program (a master's program in economics for Latin American students) in Santiago. His most recent publications include *Macro Adjustment and Public Finance* for the United Nations and *Macroeconomics of Public Sector Deficits: The Case of Chile* for the World Bank. He has contributed to a number of books on privatization, as well.

John Moore was a minister in the British cabinet from the beginning of Margaret Thatcher's Conservative government until July 1989. He entered the Cabinet in May 1986 as secretary of state for transport and, among other things, oversaw the privatization of British Airways. In 1986, he was president of the European Economic Community's Council of Transport Ministers. From 1983 to 1986 he was financial secretary to the Treasury, with responsibility for the Inland Revenue and the government's Privatisation Programme. For his work on this he was presented the Free Enterprise Award for Aims of Industry.

Ijaz Nabi is a senior economist at the World Bank, where he has worked on Mexico and Malaysia. He has published in the fields of agriculture, industry, and finance. His most recent publication is *Transitions in Development: The Role of Aid and Commercial Flows,* edited jointly with Uma Lele.

David Newbery has been director of the department of applied economics at Cambridge University and professor of applied economics since 1988. He was with the World Bank for two years as division chief of the Public Economics division. His current research interests are in public policy, regulation, electricity, environment, road pricing, the economic transformation of Eastern Europe, taxation, development economics, and economic theory.

Manuel Sanchez is professor at the Autonomous Mexican Institute of Technology (ITAM) and is also director of the Center for Economic Analysis and Research (CAIE) in Mexico.

Mary Shirley is chief of the Finance and Private Sector Development division of the World Bank. Previously, she was the World Bank's public enterprise adviser. She is the author of several World Bank studies on state-owned enterprises and numerous country studies. She previously held positions in the Bank's Latin America and Caribbean Programs, the Organization of American States, the University of Bogota, and the Harvard Economic Research Center.

Donald R. Snodgrass is an institute fellow at the Harvard Institute for International Development and lecturer on economics at Harvard University. He has served in the Economic Planning Unit of the Prime Minister's Department in Malaysia and helped to found and develop the Center for Policy and Implementation Studies, a government-sponsored policy research unit in Malaysia. He has published numerous articles and reviews on development subjects and is author or coauthor of four books, including the widely used textbook *Economics of Development.* His current research interests include small and medium-scale industry, rural banking, and economic development in Southeast Asia.

Lawrence H. Summers is under secretary for International Affairs in the U. S. Department of the Treasury. The views expressed in this article are, however, those of the author and do not represent the Department of the Treasury or the U.S. government. He was formerly vice president for Development Economics and chief economist at the World Bank.

Pankaj Tandon is associate professor of economics and an associate in the public enterprise program at Boston University. His primary research interests are in the fields of public enterprise and the economics of technological change. He has written numerous scholarly articles, and his first book (coauthored with Leroy Jones and Ingo Vogelsang) is on the privatization of public enterprises.

Ingo Vogelsang is a professor of economics at Boston University. He has written six books and monographs and many articles on public utility regulation, public enterprises, and institutional problems in energy and telecommunications. His latest books include *Public Enterprises in Monopolistic and Oligopolistic Industries, Selling Public Enterprises: A Cost-Benefit Methodology,* and *Telecommunications Pricing: Theory and Practice.* He is currently working on issues of optimal telephone tariffs, incentive regulation, and the privatization of public enterprises. His major consultancies include the RAND Corporation and the World Bank.

PART 1

THE CONTEXT

1

OVERVIEW

Ahmed Galal and Mary Shirley

This volume summarizes the presentations at a two-day World Bank conference on the welfare effects of privatization, held in Washington, D.C. on June 11-12, 1992, and attended by some 100 senior policymakers, academics, and advisers from around the world. Its objective was to disseminate the findings of two years of research conducted by the Bank and Boston University analyzing twelve cases of privatization of state-owned enterprises in four countries. The detailed analysis of the case studies will be available in a forthcoming World Bank publication. Meanwhile, this volume provides a preview and an overview of the research project and shares some of the insights of the discussants at the conference.

Privatization is an idea whose time has clearly come. Privatization is now a fact of life almost everywhere in the world. More than 7,000 enterprises have been privatized worldwide, some 2,000 of them in developing countries. Many countries have privatization plans and programs in the works that will push these numbers even higher. Despite all this activity, however, debate still rages over the impact of privatization, over how much to privatize, over how to do it and how fast to do it, and even over whether to do it. So far, most evidence has been anecdotal at best, ideological at worst, and always partial— looking perhaps at profits or at productivity, but not at the whole picture. Few systematic attempts have been made to measure the impact of privatization, and no rigorous attempts have been made to measure it *comprehensively*.

There is a host of questions about privatization that partial analyses cannot answer: If profits went up after privatization, what happened to prices? If productivity went up, what happened to labor? If the government got revenue from the sale, did it get as much as the company was worth? And, most important, what was the bottom line? Was the country better off thanks to privatization or not? Who won and who lost?

The research reported on in this volume provides some answers. The researchers analyze not just profits, but also productivity, not just the welfare gains to the economy and the benefits to workers, government, consumers, and even competitors, but also the effects on the losers. This volume provides further insights, assessments, and criticisms of the research from noted practitioners and theorists in the field.

A comprehensive approach has its limitations. Because it is costly in time, with a ravenous appetite for data, the approach can be applied only for a few countries and companies. The twelve cases reported here include three telecommunications firms, four airlines, two electricity companies, a transport company, a lottery, and a container terminal in four countries: Chile, Malaysia, Mexico, and the United Kingdom. Most of the sample enterprises (nine of twelve) are monopolies or oligopolies; all the countries are middle income or developed. Whether the results would be different in other kinds of industries and countries remains an open question. And even this comprehensive approach may not be comprehensive enough for some. Many of the discussants asked for more of what the researchers termed "atmospherics." How did privatization affect the willingness of investors to invest? How did it affect the commitment of governments to good behavior? Did it tilt the balance of political and economic power toward market-friendly policies?

Notwithstanding these limitations, the findings are striking. The bottom line? Privatization can bring substantial gains. In eleven of twelve cases, the gains were positive and large, amounting to an average 2.5 percent permanent increase in GDP. These gains are only attainable, however, if privatization is properly done. And "properly done" means that policymakers provide no special concessions or privileges when selling public enterprises, introduce competition wherever possible, and regulate monopolies.

That is not to say that the findings are applicable everywhere. In low-income countries with distorted markets and in economies in transition from central planning to competition, additional safeguards may be necessary and the gains from privatization may be different. Some of the conference participants—Larry Summers and Nancy Birdsall, to name two—argued that the gains might be much higher in low-income countries. Countries in the sample had an extraordinarily high capacity to manage enterprises well under public ownership. In countries that manage their public firms much less well and where public enterprises compound the distortions in many markets, the benefits from privatization could be huge. But these same commentators also wondered whether it might not be much harder for low-income countries to implement privatization. Since policies in these countries often lack credibility, private investors, fearing renationalization or exploitation, might offer very low prices for public enterprises. The absence of the right economic and institutional framework—a competitive private sector, an effective regulatory body—could also keep privatization from working.

But even if these types of countries are excepted, there remain many countries around the world that resemble those analyzed. And the researchers have, in fact, stacked the deck against privatization: the analysis assumes that had the enterprises remained public, they would have behaved just as the privatized companies did, unless there is strong evidence to the contrary. Further, the fact that most of the sample enterprises are monopolies should bias the results against gains from privatization, given the large potential welfare losses likely from exploitation of market power under private ownership.

That the research found substantial gains from privatizing regulated monopolies was a striking finding. Several reasons were given for this outcome and commented on by many of the participants. For one thing, all the countries regulated the private monopolies in ways that reduced or eliminated the chances to exploit consumers. For another, the shift to private ownership allowed other beneficial changes to occur: an increase in investment (British Telecom, Chile Telecom), a rise in prices toward levels that reflect scarcity values (British Telecom, Telmex, Malaysian Airline Systems), greater productivity thanks to managerial effort (Kelang Container Terminal in Malaysia, Chile's electricity generation, CHILGENER), better marketing and diversification (Malaysian Lottery, Chile

Telecom), and the freedom to shed excess labor (Aeromexico, British Telecom).

This volume presents the results of the case studies and the debate on the research design, assumptions, and analysis by theorists and practitioners familiar with the cases studied. The opening remarks by Larry Summers lay out major lessons from the research for the World Bank and the rest of the international community. Summers argues that the research shows much more conclusively than previous analyses that ownership matters. But privatization can be hard to accomplish, partly because the gains are diffuse while the costs are highly visible and concentrated. Summers defines the problem of the "privatization trap." Because buyers do not trust governments not to intervene, they will pay less for the enterprises than they otherwise would. Then if the government does behave well, the buyers reap a windfall gain, creating pressures for the government to misbehave and confirming their worst suspicions. One of the challenges facing international agencies is to free governments from this trap, overcome the biases against privatization, and help countries realize the gains.

Before the presentations on the methodology and case studies, Roger Douglas details some of the lessons he finds in New Zealand's experience with privatization. The primary lesson is the need to be very clear about what privatization is expected to achieve. In New Zealand the objective was very explicitly competition, and the desire to achieve more competitive markets drove most of the decisions about privatization. Following from that lesson is the need to ensure that the regulatory environment and competition policies are right before enterprises are sold. And finally, enterprise reform must be a part of a much wider pattern of structural change.

The lead researcher, Leroy Jones, follows Douglas's presentation with a thumbnail sketch of the research method: the questions asked (who won, who lost, and how much) and the techniques used to find the answers. This deceptively simple introduction gradually sketches the comprehensive and complex methodology developed to quantify how much of a difference privatization makes.

The case studies begin with Ingo Vogelsang's presentation of the pacesetting privatizer, the United Kingdom. British Telecom is one of his most controversial and demanding cases, as the reactions of his discussants show. John Moore was in the Conservative government when the privatization occurred, and his remarks highlight the importance the government attached to denationalization. Moore takes issue with Vogelsang's assumption that public pressure would eventually have forced the British Government to boost its investments in British Telecom had it remained in public hands. Relaxing that assumption would push the very substantial gains recorded from privatizing British Telecom even higher (because privatization would be assumed to have made an even bigger difference). David Newbery's comments focus on the importance of the regulatory framework when utilities such as British Telecom are privatized, noting the U.K.'s success in building credible regulatory institutions (and avoiding Summers's privatization trap).

The Chilean cases presented by Ahmed Galal deal with two monopolies and one quasi competitive firm. The three firms were well regulated and well run before they were privatized. Yet privatization still yielded important gains. Jorge Marshall speculates that the gains from privatization could be much higher in countries that have not reformed their public enterprises. Like Moore with Vogelsang, Marshall, a member of the government of Chile, takes issue with Galal's assumption that the government of Chile would have invested in Chile Telecom had the company not been privatized. But Rolf Luders, who was minister of finance in the Pinochet government, argues that the investment would have been made. Luders suggests computing probability distributions for the counterfactuals to clarify their speculative nature.

The Mexican cases presented by Pankaj Tandon are strikingly different from those for the United Kingdom and Chile. These were not well run companies. One of the airlines was a major drain on the budget, and the other companies, though less spectacularly bad, were nonetheless poor performers. The gains to Mexico from privatization were substantial, not only directly, but also because privatization was a central part of a broader program of liberalization. Manuel Sanchez identifies some of the risks in the research methodology when applied to the Mexico cases, one being the risk of treating as causal factors, that merely occur contemporaneously with privatization.

Leroy Jones introduces the Malaysian cases saying "welcome to the real world." Malaysia's smaller privatization program with its many partial sales is more typical of privatization in most developing countries, which he calculates have sold an average of only five companies each. His three cases consist of competitive companies, which make up the bulk of enterprises sold, but a minority of those in the sample. Ijaz Nabi prefaces his comments by asking a larger question that the case studies do not answer: How did privatization contribute to the overall efficiency and competitiveness of the economy? And like other discussants, he takes issue with the tricky question of how to construct the counterfactual. David Snodgrass puts the privatization program in the context of Malaysia's efforts to promote ethnic peace and fairness. He notes that even though gains in economic welfare may not be the government's primary objective for privatization, such gains may still result, even in the politically complex conditions of countries like Malaysia.

The volume moves then from the country cases to general findings. Jones presents the patterns of winners and losers, and Galal assess the policy implications. Nancy Birdsall reacts to these global findings, pointing out the unanswered questions, the missing pieces of the privatization jigsaw puzzle. Birdsall calls for more research, particularly on the implications for poor economies and the former command economies, which may be in a low-level equilibrium unconducive to privatization. David Newbery notes that basic economic theory tells us that privatization should not make a difference in performance. He then proceeds to discuss why it might make the difference found in these cases.

Joining Birdsall, two of the final panelists call for more research. Heba Handoussa notes that government intervention will not disappear overnight in developing countries and calls for more study to determine what is the minimum amount of intervention needed. Rolf Luders points out that the methodology used for this research could also be used before the sale to assess the impact of different methods of sale. Finally, Johannes Linn presents a wish list for future research, including examination of the sustainability of sound regulation over time, and the impact of the culture of management on the results. Noting that the failure of this research to provide unequivocal answers and instructions may disappoint some people, Linn argues that a narrow definition of the questions and a careful delimitation of the applicability of the answers is the hallmark of good research.

2

A CHANGING COURSE TOWARD PRIVATIZATION

Lawrence H. Summers

There is a story about the U.S. Navy that, I think, captures the way many governments feel about confronting market forces. A Navy fleet is sailing in the Pacific when a blip appears on the fleet's radar screen. The destroyer's captain sends the message: "We are on a collision course, change your course." The reply comes back: "Change your course." Irritated, the captain sends another message: "This is the U.S. Navy's fleet. We are on a collision course. Change your course." Again the reply: "Change your course." Finally, the admiral of the U.S. fleet, thoroughly annoyed, sends the message: "This is the most powerful sailing force ever assembled. We are on a collision course. Change your course." Comes the reply: "Change your course. This is a lighthouse."

Some forces are inevitable, and surely one of them is the pressure on governments to move toward competitive market systems over the next decade. The research being examined at this conference is fundamentally important because it moves the discussion of privatization beyond ideology and anecdote to analysis. Now it is true that a study with a set of twelve case studies might tempt some to trot out the old chestnut that "data" are the pleural of "anecdote." But I think that the kind of comparisons being made are important and striking nonetheless. For a set of countries with an abnormally high capacity to manage public enterprises in a set of sectors where the case for public enterprises is strongest, these studies nonetheless find

The author is under secretary for international affairs, Department of the Treasury, the United States of America. The views expressed in this article are, however, those of the author and do not represent the Department of the Treasury or the U.S. government.

significant improvements following privatization in nearly all cases. Of course, the sample is small and special, but I think it is likely that for governments that are less capable and for industries that are more exposed to competition, the gains from privatization will be greater, not smaller, than those found in this research.

Four very important lessons for World Bank policy and for those involved in supporting reform in developing countries emerge from this research. I will comment briefly on them and then present a few concluding thoughts on the privatization question.

Ownership and Competition

First, it is ownership, in addition to market conditions, that is decisive in determining performance in the public sector. It is not obvious that markets feel any difference between bad and good ownership, public or private ownership. Nor is it obvious how ownership should change with the degree of competition. After all, it is possible that where there is competition, enterprises will be disciplined in any event, and that where there is no competition, ownership and capital market discipline become more important and can make a greater difference in improving performance.

The before-and-after comparisons of this research seem to provide much stronger evidence than the typical cross-sectional comparisons that try, but never completely succeed, to hold everything else constant when measuring the relative efficiency of private and public ownership. Of course, those who criticize a view that emphasizes private ownership will argue that there are well-functioning, efficient public enterprises in many parts of the world. But in making a judgment about what policy conclusion to draw from that reality, it seems to me that that observation has to be tempered by several others.

For one thing, these successes are often ephemeral, particularly when they are the result of public enterprise reform programs. I find especially striking Mary Shirley's observation that the 1983 *World Development Report* on which she worked highlighted a wide variety of successes in public enterprise reform, most of which have since gone wrong and are no longer thought of as successes.

And even if public enterprises sometimes succeed, the question is whether they succeed in an expected-value sense. How many cases are there in which we can be confident in advance that performance will be better in enterprises in the public sector than in those in the private sector, given the track record? It is not enough to observe that the distributions of public and private enterprise performance overlap. To make a policy-relevant case requires finding instances in which the conditional mean, if you will, of the distribution of public enterprise performance is higher than the conditional mean for the private sector. I think that it has not yet been demonstrated that there are many cases that meet that criterion.

A last point—and the most important—is that the instances in which public enterprises succeed are typically the instances in which it makes the least difference whether the enterprise is public or private. The successes do not take the form in which the public sector, freed of the need to maximize profits, somehow achieves other objectives more satisfactorily, doing things the private sector would be unable to do. Nor are the successes cases in which the enterprise operates not only very efficiently, but also more equitably than the private enterprise would. The successes, whether in France or Singapore, are the cases in which the public enterprise functions just like a private company would. That implies that whatever the general benefits of public ownership might be thought to be, the government is, in fact, not reaping those benefits to any very substantial extent and could indeed receive the same fiscal benefits by selling off its claim to the profits.

I think the right presumption for approaching reform is that ownership does matter. And this research illustrates that we should maintain a strong presumption in favor of moving as many enterprises to the private sector as rapidly as possible. As the authors of the study acknowledge, calculations of the benefits of privatization are unable to measure one very important aspect. When governments are no longer involved in managing enterprises, administrative capacity that once went toward that activity is freed to work toward other activities that only governments can perform.

Reflections on Difficulties in Privatization

A second lesson concerns the difficulties of privatization. Is privatization difficult? Yes. But in thinking about whether privatization is desirable, concerns about the difficulties frequently lead to the wrong conclusion: let's not do it. Like other policy issues, privatization is surely a matter of comparisons among options.

Some governments will have less capacity to regulate enterprises than others, but I would venture to suggest that the governments with the least capacity to regulate enterprises are the governments with the least capacity to operate enterprises. It is also the case that some countries have less-developed capital markets, making privatization more difficult. But the governments of those countries will have even more difficulty raising capital to finance the deficits associated with the inevitable subsidies to public enterprises. And some governments will have less capacity or less political ability to put in place satisfactory safety net programs, but once again it is often those governments, bowing to political pressures, that do the least to see that public enterprises help the genuinely poor rather than their upper middle-class employees.

In thinking about privatization, I would suggest that we need much less of a status quo bias. We have a strong tendency to pose the question: "Can we privatize this enterprise in a satisfactory way?" rather than: "Was it a mistake to nationalize this enterprise fifteen years ago, and if so, should that mistake be reversed?" The question is one of comparison. Arguments of the form "the less well-developed the institutional environment in the country, the less strong the case for privatization," seem to me to be wrong. For the same reasons that privatization will be difficult, operation in the public sector will be even more difficult.

Potential Biases against Privatization

Third, there are inherent political biases against privatization that donors should seek to counteract. There is every reason to think that national governments, free of external pressure, will underprivatize rather than overprivatize. Our weight should therefore come down on the privatization side of the scale.

There is the obvious point of inertia. It takes a conscious effort, a conscious strategy, to move enterprises from the public sector to the private sector. But there is also a more subtle, and probably more important point. The costs of privatization are very visible, which makes it possible to accuse the privatizer of giving away the crown jewels. But the benefits of privatization are much less visible. The consumers who benefit and the workers who are hired because the now-private company has the capacity to expand do not say to themselves two years later: "Thank goodness this enterprise was privatized; otherwise, I wouldn't have been able to buy these goods so cheaply or get this job." They credit their employment to their own initiative and success. The losers will be angry and the winners will probably be ungrateful since they will have little inclination to trace the benefits back to privatization. And that also creates a political bias toward too little action.

That bias is reinforced by the way many public enterprises got where they are. In too many countries, substantial external financial support has long been available for state enterprises but not for private enterprises. Not surprisingly, that has created a bias in favor of keeping state enterprises in the state sector.

All these factors—inertia, the distribution of benefits, external support—have created biases in the political process that make it likely that decisions will give too much weight to the cost of privatization and too little to the benefits. These biases are intensified by the common phenomenon that managers of both private and public firms—and ministries—tend to want to expand their sphere of control (causing companies to worry more about expanding and less about profitability).

Privatization and Other Reforms: The Privatization Trap

Fourth, privatization has to be combined appropriately with other policy reforms. The worst sin, and probably the most common, is to use privatization for a quick revenue fix: selling the firm to capture today the benefits of future revenues. Price and regulatory concessions become part of the privatization package, even though there is no case at all for making special concessions in order to privatize. There is a case for laying down clearly and precisely what the rules of the game will be so that a fair auction can take place, with bids based on judgments about what investment can do rather than on what government regulatory policies will be.

There is a phenomenon that helps explain why privatization often moves slowly. I refer to it as the privatization trap. Imagine a government that historically—for whatever reasons—has not been credibly committed to capitalist policies. Now imagine that the government is trying to sell an enterprise. Because of the government's record, buyers will be wary, and the enterprise will not fetch a high price. There are two possibilities after that: the government will live up to the buyer's fears and the enterprise will be regulated to death, or the government will behave honorably and keep its hands off. Now in the latter case those who purchased the asset will receive an enormous windfall, and that will create pressures for the government to reverse itself and expropriate some of the gains. So a government that lacks credibility has a very real problem: it can't get a fair price for the sale of the asset and behave properly too. If it behaves properly, then the buyer gets a windfall; if it doesn't behave properly, then it gets more out of the deal but it didn't behave properly. With this type of situation, there is a tendency toward drift in the hope that the government's credibility will improve later, and the enterprise will fetch a higher price. But what usually happens is that the price falls even more over time, because without a clearly articulated privatization policy and program neither the government's credibility nor its performance improves.

What can be done? I don't have a fully satisfactory answer to that question, but two thoughts suggest themselves. The most obvious is to sell a part of the enterprise and transfer most of the control. A subsequent sale of the remaining assets can reap the benefits of credibility—higher prices—once it has been earned. The second, which may have more merit than might first appear, is to transfer ownership under a long-term lease. Several Latin American countries have privatized firms this way. The first reaction is to consider the option crazy: as the end of the lease nears, won't there be an incentive not to invest, to run down the assets? But if you can't sell an enterprise's profits fifteen years down the line for a positive price today, why give them away today? Why not retain some rights and try to sell them in the future, when a positive price can be collected? The privatization trap captures a significant part of the reason governments move so slowly. We need to think about what can be done to mitigate that problem.

Where Do We Go from Here?

The policy lessons that flow from this study are strong enough to bring to an end the kind of research agnosticism that has been common in the donor community. These lessons support a very strong presumption against providing assistance to state enterprises that face potential competition and could be privatized. And these lessons justify strong pressures from donors for privatization, including exploring ways to provide foreign assistance directly to privatized enterprises. Eligibility for assistance need not reside exclusively in the state sector.

While there has been enough research to generate policy conclusions strong enough for the donor community to act on, there is clearly a need for more. Part of it will take the form of applying the valuable methodology developed in this study to a wider variety of contexts, and perhaps of devising techniques to apply the methodology to reprivatizations, to evaluate the possible consequences of privatizations. Also, we need to look harder than we have at the distributional consequences of privatization. My prediction is that the case against privatization on income distribution grounds will turn out to be very weak. If one's views on distribution are driven by concern for the poor, it will be a rare privatization in which the poor are found to be significant losers. There will probably still be some privatizations that will make some people very rich, and the ethical defense of that wealth will be difficult to achieve. But if, as I believe, issues of income distribution are best approached through concern for the poor rather than envy of the wealthy, these results will not prove to be such a serious problem.

I want to commend the authors and those who commissioned this study for a first-rate piece of work. I am confident it will influence the debate on this issue for years to come.

3

PRIVATIZATION: LESSONS FROM NEW ZEALAND

Roger Douglas

The presentations at this conference will provide answers to many of the questions swirling around privatization: Who won and who lost? Where did the gains and losses come from? What made divestiture a positive- or a negative-sum game? In my presentation, I will address these questions from a political perspective, against the background of my New Zealand experience.

Know What You Want To Do

What does that experience tell us? Lesson number one is the need to be very clear about objectives. In New Zealand competition was the primary objective. We were prepared to sacrifice price to get maximum competition. Still, we almost always sought to obtain the highest price we could for the government assets we sold. And we often succeeded.

Lesson two is in many ways the most important—and the most difficult. Unless the government is prepared to deal with staffing issues—the number of employees, staff privileges, and the like—privatization is not likely to succeed. For example, we reduced staff in New Zealand Telecom from 27,000 to 12,000 in three years and achieved productivity levels in nine months that it took three years to attain in the United Kingdom. Yet wherever I have looked, from Russia to Brazil to Pakistan, most governments seem ill-prepared to tackle the labor problem.

Lesson three is that competition drives innovation, providing the impetus for seeking new and better ways of doing things. But wherever there is competition, there is risk. And the question that then arises is who should be taking that risk? Should governments force

19

their taxpayers into the front lines in the major battles between rivals in the commercial airline or telecommunication businesses?

Consider the case of Air New Zealand. The airline is a state-owned business that had always done a first-class job for customers on the international routes. It had to, because it was competing with Pan Am, Quantas, British Airways, and others. But at home, where it had a domestic monopoly, the story was different. Passengers were forced to trudge through good and bad weather from the terminal to the aircraft; they had to wait twenty to thirty minutes at the other end for their luggage. Domestic passengers didn't realize what they were missing until the government decided to break Air New Zealand's monopoly and let another airline work the domestic routes alongside Air New Zealand. Overnight, to our amazement, we found that we too, the New Zealand public, could have protected passage to planes just like the rest of the world did. Since the end of World War II a prefabricated building had been used as a terminal in Wellington, and in all that time no one had been able to get it upgraded. Now, suddenly, we had totally modern terminal buildings. We also got more flights, cheaper flights, better food, friendlier service, and virtually no waiting time for our luggage. And people began to see that the central issue in safeguarding their interests as consumers was competition.

The Air New Zealand case also illustrates my first lesson: that governments have to be clear about their objective at the outset. Air New Zealand was on the list of enterprises to be sold, but by allowing another airline to come in as a competitor, we clearly reduced the sales value of Air New Zealand to the government as a shareholder. But you have to ask, what are you trying to accomplish? Are we aiming primarily to improve the value of Air New Zealand, or is our main aim to give passengers and shippers of air freight a better deal that improves economic activity? We chose the latter.

Lesson four is to ensure that the regulatory environment and competition policies are right before you privatize. If that cannot be done for some reason—and there may be valid reasons for that—then give notice that the policies will change and that they will change in a way that encourages maximum competition. Then the buyer enters into the purchase with eyes open.

Another point that is recognized indirectly in the case study papers is the importance of people. We found in New Zealand that the success of our program depended as much on people as it did on policy. In most cases the existing management either wanted to take over the business or pushed for widespread share ownership rather than sale to a strategic buyer, someone with money on the line who wanted to improve performance. In most cases, we sold to a strategic buyer.

Sixth, state enterprise reform should be only one part of a much wider pattern of structural change. Any comprehensive program of economic restructuring will inevitably create winners and losers. If the program is comprehensive, the losers will generally be those who are receiving existing privileges—and they will lose them permanently. In my view, these people should not generally receive compensation. The people who should receive some compensation are those who really have no ability to do much about the costs of restructuring. For example, in Russia I would put the retired population in that category. People in that category need to be protected.

Wherever possible, reform should be packaged so that losers in one area become winners in another. And when dismantling privileges is the order of the day, government needs an overall program that defines objectives clearly and allows movement toward them in what I call quantum leaps. Otherwise, the interest groups have time to mobilize, and they will drag down the reforms.

In New Zealand, and probably everywhere else in the world, the conventional perception about reformers is that they are playing against a stacked deck of cards. Privatization as part of genuine structural reform is portrayed as the equivalent of political suicide. That view is probably accurate when privileges are removed one at a time in a step-by-step program. Paradoxically, it ceases to apply when the privileges of many groups are removed at once. In that case, individual groups may lose their special privileges, but they benefit simultaneously because the aggregate cost of paying for the privileges of all the other groups is lifted. It is also harder to complain about damage to your own group's interests when everyone else is suffering at least as much—and you are benefiting from their loss in the medium term.

Do It Quickly and Forthrightly

In any program of structural reform it is uncertainty, not speed, that endangers success. In New Zealand, many apparent demands for a slower pace were, in fact, expressions of a powerful resentment that the government was not moving fast enough to abolish privileges enjoyed by rival groups.

Speed, then, is essential for keeping uncertainty down to the lowest achievable levels. When state trading departments were being transferred to commercial corporations, it became apparent that there would be large-scale staff redundancies in forestry and coal. In fact, in one day the forestry staff in New Zealand dropped from 7,000 people to 2,700. Because some of the jobs were located in depressed areas, the government took its time making the final decisions, leaving thousands of employees in limbo for six months. Employees knew that some of them had no future in the industry, but no one knew who they were. So no one could leave before the government made up its mind because then they might lose their severance pay. The result was deep and intense bitterness, which the government interpreted as a response to the policies themselves. That further eroded the willingness to act decisively. Once the government made firm decisions and announced them, however, the feeling in the regions improved rapidly. The people had long known that change was inevitable. Indeed, the public often showed more realism than the politicians. What the people really wanted was an end to the uncertainty so that they could get on with their lives.

Be Consistent and Steadfast

Another lesson is that consistency plus credibility equal economic confidence. An unbroken record of credibility is essential for maintaining public confidence in any structural reform program and, I might emphasize, for minimizing the cost. The key to credibility is consistency of policy and communication. When governments lack credibility, people refuse to change until the clash between their old behavior and the new policy imperatives has imposed large, unavoidable costs on the economy. As a reform program rolls forward, a lot of people are hurt. Their confidence in the program depends on maintaining the conviction that the government will drive the reform program through to its successful conclusion. Speed, momentum, the avoidance of spur-of-the-moment decisions, and an unwavering consistency in serving medium-term objectives are the crucial ingredients for establishing credibility.

Structural reform has its own internal logic. That logic is based on the linkages within the economy: one step inevitably requires that the next one be taken if benefits are to be extracted for the nation as a whole. That is certainly what we found in New Zealand. Once we started down the path of structural reform, that reform took on its own momentum, its own particular logic.

Finally, successful structural reform does not become possible until the government trusts, respects, and informs the public. Voters need to be in a position to make sound judgments about what is going on. The public needs to be told right up front, and told regularly, what the problem is and how it came about, what damage it is doing to their own personal interests, what the objectives are in tackling it, how the government intends to achieve those objectives, and what the costs and benefits of that action will be. People need to be told about the costs as well as the benefits. And, of course, they need to be told why the government's approach is better than anyone else's.

PART 2

APPROACH
AND CASE STUDIES

4

QUESTIONS
AND APPROACHES TO ANSWERS

Leroy Jones

In conducting our study, we developed a common methodology and applied it to all the case studies. The details of this methodology will become clearer in the discussions of the case studies, especially Ingo Vogelsang's discussion of the British Telecom case. I want to present an overview of the methodology here, identifying the distinguishing characteristics of the study and the questions we sought to answer, and explaining how we attempted to answer them. I will conclude by mentioning some of the methodological tradeoffs that we faced.

Characteristics of the Study

This is an empirical study. We don't simply tell stories; we quantify all our findings. The focus is on case studies, and on case studies of companies not countries. We do not try to evaluate the privatization programs or strategies of the countries in the sample except as they are manifested in the case studies. To be sure, we have something to say about those programs. But that is not the focus. The focus is on what happened in individual companies.

We are concerned particularly with the change in welfare and how much the nation and the world gained or lost from the divestiture. Getting the real picture requires taking a comprehensive view of divestiture. It is not enough to look only at bits and pieces, say only at total factor productivity or only at private profits. It is also important to look at the total change in welfare and its distribution among workers, consumers, government, buyers of the firm, competitors, and a broader mass of the citizens. Finally, finding out about how things changed as a result of the divestiture decision requires asking what happened that would not have happened without the divestiture—the counterfactual case.

Questions

Thus, the basic questions then are: Who won, who lost, and how much? Answering these questions requires answering four subsidiary questions first.

- The factual question: What happened to the company before and after divestiture? We typically take a five-year history of the company before and (ideally) after divestiture and compare the two periods to see what, if anything, changed after divestiture.
- The counterfactual: How much of the change would have occurred without the divestiture—how much can actually be attributed to divestiture and how much to exogenous factors?
- The simulations: What are the welfare results when the factual and the counterfactual are projected into the future?
- The valuation of the difference: How much difference did divestiture make?

The Sample

Our sample is not random (table 4.1). It is concentrated by type of industry (three telecommunications firms, four airlines, two electricity companies, and three odds-and-ends firms—truck transport, a lottery, and a container terminal) and by market structure (nine of the twelve companies are monopolies or oligopolies).

The heavy representation of monopoly or oligopoly firms was intentional, since the bulk of output of public enterprises in most countries is produced by monopolies or oligopolies. In addition, one of the most important determinants of the success of divestiture is market conditions.

The sample focuses on the most problematic issues of divestiture. The theoretical argument for having public enterprises in the first place is to avoid exploitation of consumers by monopolies. Governments have two ways of dealing with monopoly power: public ownership, or private ownership with regulation. The interesting question is which is the least costly way. When governments divest

Table 4.1 The Sample

Country and Company	Sector	Market Share (%)	Size (1000 employees)	Year of Divestiture
UNITED KINGDOM				
British Telecom	Telecommunications	97	235.0	1984
British Airways	Airlines	39	40.8	1987
National Freight	Truck transport	10	24.3	1982
MALAYSIA				
Malaysian Airlines	Airlines	60	10.6	1985
Kelang Container	Container terminal	55	0.8	1986
Sports Toto	Lotter	5	0.4	1985
MEXICO				
Telmex	Telecommunications	100	50.0	1990
Mexicana	Airlines	50	12.7	1989
Aeromexico	Airlines	50	11.5	1988
CHILE				
Chilgener	Electricity generation	13	0.8	1987
Enersis	Electricity distribution	95	2.5	1987
CTC	Telecommunications	95	7.2	1988

Source: Galal, Ahmed, Leroy Jones, Pankaj Tandon, and Ingo Vogelsang, *Welfare Consequences of Selling Public Enterprises: Case Studies from Chile, Malaysia, Mexico and the United Kingdom* (New York: Oxford University Press, forthcoming).

monopolies and oligopolies, there is at least the possibility that divestiture would make consumers worse off. In other words, divestiture can involve a fundamental tradeoff between improving efficiency in the private sector and increasing exploitation of consumers.

A major constraint in the selection process was the need for cases with a long enough history before, and especially after, divestiture. Despite all the interest in divestiture in recent years, it was difficult to find four countries with a substantial number of companies that had been divested long enough ago to have a post-divestiture history. Because the sample was not random, there is sample bias. That bias affects the extent to which the results can be generalized to other countries and other companies.

Methodology

The research sought to answer the questions posed above by first establishing what happened to the company before and after divestiture. To this end, we used a methodology that we called "kink interoccular impact analysis." That is, we looked at the trend, looked for a kink in it big enough to hit us between the eyes, and looked for turning points associated with the kink.

Next, we developed the counterfactual scenario to see how much of the change was attributable to divestiture. A common problem is that countries generally decide to divest during recession, when times are bad. That happened in all our sample countries. By the time divestiture takes place some two years later, the economy is turning around. So we try to determine how much of the company's upturn is due to the privatization and improved management and how much would have taken place anyway because of the improving economy.

Our next concern was to project the changes into the future. Many of the changes associated with divestiture, particularly for a large firm, do not manifest themselves immediately. No one is going to change British Telecom, a company with 240,000 employees, overnight. Many of the benefits of divestiture emerge down the line, as a result of better planning, better management, and more forward-looking behavior. As with other aspects of the analysis, we were conservative in projecting trends. Whenever we had a choice, we tried to come down on the conservative side, erring in favor of decisions that would minimize projected benefits.

We looked not only at the profits of the enterprise, but also at the profits earned by competitors in the market, including foreigners, and at consumer surplus. We identified profits and consumer surplus in up to a dozen commodities, analyzing them separately for each commodity, for each year, and for the factual and counterfactual. Profit, or the bottom line, depends on whose interests are being reflected. Private profit is measured to reflect the interests of the equity holder, and hence excludes a large number of returns to capital—returns to government's claim on capital, debt payers' claim on capital, and a few other things. So we also measured profit in the context of capital owned by all of society—what economists call quasi rents and we called public profit, to contrast with private profit. Simply put, public profit is the value of output after deducting all intermediate input costs, employee compensation, factor rentals, the opportunity cost of working capital, in other words, total return to capital.

Dividing the total return to capital by fixed capital yields profitability. Doing this in constant prices provides a measure of efficiency that is close to a measure of total factor productivity. The case studies talk about efficiency changes and efficiency gains, often measured in terms of public profitability at costs in constant prices or in terms of total factor productivity. Either way, they generally measure about the same thing.

The last question is valuation, or how we add things up. We add things up so that our global measure of welfare change is equal to the change in consumer and producer surplus, plus changes in the rents earned by competitors. Then we apportion the change in welfare among the various actors. We know what goes to consumers, labor, and competitors, but what about profit? Profit is divided between the government as seller and the private buyer, with each side's share determined by how well each bargained beforehand on the price of the firm. The buyer's share is reflected by the present value of the future returns of the company, appropriately discounted, less the purchase price. With a purchase price of say $100 and a present value of future returns at 10 percent of $100, the purchaser does not come out ahead. The purchaser gets normal profits, but the returns are zero—there are no rents. However, if discounted future returns exceed the purchase price, rents are generated and the purchaser comes out ahead. The total change in profits less what the buyer gets goes to government as the government's share.

If the economy is in a fiscal or balance of payments crisis at the time of divestiture, money in government hands may be particularly valuable because it can be used to alleviate the crisis. We reflect that premium on government revenue with a multiplier, a shadow price on government revenue relative to some shadow price on private revenue. The Telmex sale in Mexico is a case in point.

Conclusion

If we simply want to know what happens to private profit, that is relatively easy to determine. If we want to know what happens to productivity, that is more complicated: we need more numbers and there are some estimation problems. If we want to know what happens to consumer surplus, we have even bigger problems: we need to know elasticities, and we need to resolve some theoretical issues about the meaning of consumer surplus. If we want to examine the counterfactual, then we need to make hypothetical judgments. Finally, we have to project these hypothetical judgments into the future. We have done all this. Thus, we have applied a very comprehensive framework that asks all the relevant questions about welfare change. All the pieces to answer the simpler questions are also there for people who are more risk averse in their research.

5

THE UNITED KINGDOM

Ingo Vogelsang

You might well wonder why the World Bank, which ordinarily deals with low-income countries, has engaged in a study of divestiture in the United Kingdom. The main reason is the country's position at the forefront of the privatization drive. We thought there was much to learn from the pacesetting country. The three cases we examine are British Telecom, British Airways, and National Freight.

Background

When the divestiture program started in the United Kingdom in 1979, the country was moving into a deep recession with high unemployment, high inflation, and a tight government budget. By 1982, the country was beginning a period of moderate growth, low inflation, and loosened budget constraints—in part, it seems, because of the privatization program.

The privatization program was a daring one. The United Kingdom divested some very large companies that generated £27 billion in sales revenue until 1990 and employed 800,000 people. As a result, the share of GDP held by public enterprises dropped by 6.5 percent. The program was innovative in many ways. For one, it was accompanied by a new form of arm's-length regulation based on a price cap, in this case the retail price index minus an efficiency factor (RPI minus x). For another, it made wide use of employee share ownership and emphasized broad share ownership in general. This characteristic was particularly prominent in the case of British Telecom. When 50 percent of the company was divested in 1984 for £3.7 billion, it was the largest flotation of any kind until that year—and the company came to have the largest number of shareholders of any company in the world.

British Telecom

The British Telecom study is an example of "kink interoccular trend analysis" par excellence. Consider profitability. Long before divestiture of British Telecom, private profitability had gone up and then down again; after divestiture, it went up again. So it looks as though divestiture has had some effect on private profitability. A similar trend holds for public profitability, except that it goes up *before* divestiture (figure 5.1).

Some of that rise may have been due to the announcement of the divestiture plan in late 1982. Management knew that things were going to get tough, that divestiture was going to occur, so they had to improve performance. But most of the boost came from the economy itself, which was turning around at the time. Other companies that remained in the public domain also did better, so this is a case in which the kink may be deceiving.

We also noted a kink in gross fixed capital formation shortly after divestiture. The United Kingdom was under severe fiscal constraints in the late 1970s and early 1980s, and even a company that was largely self-financing had difficulty getting additional funds from the treasury. Once privatized, however, British Telecom had better access to capital markets and could expand more freely. Within a short period, gross capital formation doubled. Thus, this kink pointed us to one of the direct effects of the divestiture of British Telecom: a large increase in gross capital formation.

The regulatory scheme used for British Telecom and other monopolies that were subsequently divested relied on a price cap, the RPI minus x formula. This mechanism has two main features: it holds the price level of the regulated firm below the consumer price index, and it allows the firm to rebalance its prices. The "x" factor was increased twice over the years (from 3.00 to 4.50 percent, and then to 6.25 percent). At the same time, British Telecom rebalanced its rates and reduced cross-subsidization.

That is what happened. What would have happened without divestiture? For one thing, there would have been less capital

Figure 5.1 British Telecom: What Happened? Fiscal Flows.

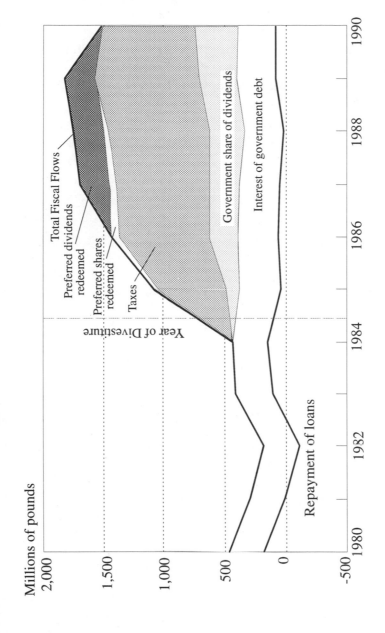

Source: Vogelsang, Ingo, with contributions from Manuel Abdala, Christopher Doyle, and Richard Green, "The United Kingdom," in Ahmed Galal, Leroy Jones, Pankaj Tandon, and Ingo Vogelsang, *Welfare Consequences of Selling Public Enterprises: Case Studies from Chile, Malaysia, Mexico and the United Kingdom* (New York: Oxford University Press, forthcoming).

accumulation, so that British Telecom would have been less able to introduce new technology. Productivity would have been only slightly lower, but even a 1 percent drop can make a big difference over time. And the innovative price cap regulation would not have been introduced.

In looking at what will happen, we tried to play it safe. We took the information we had—for example, the price cap formula for the next few years—and extrapolated trends for inflation, output prices, price levels and structures, demand development, and input productivity and prices. By making the same assumptions for the factual and the counterfactual scenarios, we expected to minimize the effects from mistakes in projections on our results.

When we add it all up, who won and who lost? In the British Telecom case the main winners are the consumers and those who purchased the stock, including employees (figure 5.2). The

Figure 5.2 British Telecom: Who Won? Who Lost?

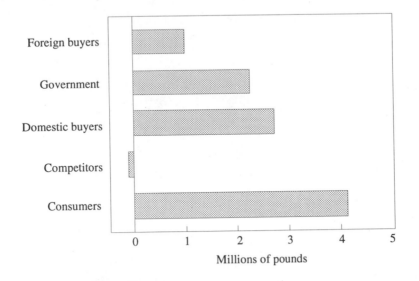

Millions of pounds

Source: Vogelsang, Ingo, with contributions from Manuel Abdala, Christopher Doyle, and Richard Green, "The United Kingdom," in Ahmed Galal, Leroy Jones, Pankaj Tandon, and Ingo Vogelsang, *Welfare Consequences of Selling Public Enterprises: Case Studies from Chile, Malaysia, Mexico and the United Kingdom* (New York: Oxford University Press, forthcoming).

government is also a moderate winner, even though it deliberately underpriced the shares to get wider share ownership, so some of the gains to government were transferred to dfomestic buyers. Competitors experienced a small loss, which means that the company is acting more aggressively.

British Airways

What distinguishes the British Airways case is the long time between the divestiture announcement in 1979 and its consummation in 1987. What further distinguishes this case is that this long delay seems to have been benign. Several factors account for that. The management that would lead the firm through divestiture was appointed early on, and the government let the firm work under arm's-length control. In the interval between the announcing and the doing, British Airways slashed its work force from 57,000 to 37,000 (in 1984).

After divestiture British Airways merged with British Caledonia, a merger unlikely to have occurred had British Airways stayed in public hands. The merger was a successful one that took advantage of the synergies between the two airlines. But British Airways' market power increased, and even a small increase in market power can be costly to consumers. The airline's market power has diminished over time, however, as new competitors entered the market, which would not have happened without the privatization.

So what is the bottom line? Consumers had a moderate loss (figure 5.3). So did competitors, but their loss is spurious because it includes the hypothetical case of British Caledonia. The main effect is a substantial gain for buyers and the government. If the effect of the announcement of the sale and the appointment of the right management is also taken into account, the gain is even greater.

National Freight

National Freight is a holding company operating in a competitive industry, truck transport. The story should be better known than it is. National Freight is a major success story of divestiture through a leveraged buy-out to employees.

Figure 5.3 British Airways: Who Won? Who Lost?

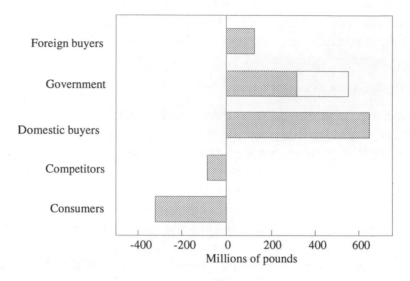

Source: Vogelsang, Ingo, with contributions from Manuel Abdala, Christopher Doyle, and Richard Green, "The United Kingdom," in Ahmed Galal, Leroy Jones, Pankaj Tandon, and Ingo Vogelsang, *Welfare Consequences of Selling Public Enterprises: Case Studies from Chile, Malaysia, Mexico and the United Kingdom* (New York: Oxford University Press, forthcoming).

Employee ownership turned out to be a boon both to the company in terms of productivity gains and to the employees in terms of capital gains and dividends. For employees who purchased shares, the capital gains alone rose to 10,000 percent or more in six to seven years. Shares bought in 1982 for £500 were worth some £50,000 in 1989.

What is the bottom line in this case (figure 5.4)? Since National Freight operates in a competitive industry, we did not measure the effect on consumers or competitors. Shareholders were the big winners. The government was a loser, although by a small amount, because the value of the assets at the time of divestiture probably exceeded the sales price.

Lessons

What can we learn from the U.K. cases? We see that the before and after comparisons generally exaggerated the effect of these divestitures. One reason is that the country was emerging from a

Figure 5.4 National Freight: Who Won? Who Lost?

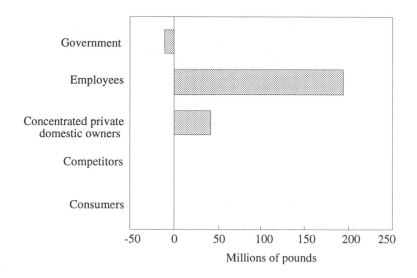

Source: Vogelsang, Ingo, with contributions from Manuel Abdala, Christopher Doyle, and Richard Green, "The United Kingdom," in Ahmed Galal, Leroy Jones, Pankaj Tandon, and Ingo Vogelsang, *Welfare Consequences of Selling Public Enterprises: Case Studies from Chile, Malaysia, Mexico and the United Kingdom* (New York: Oxford University Press, forthcoming).

recession, so there would have been some kind of positive effect in any case. Another is that we have a very demanding yardstick in our counterfactual, since the Thatcher government did a good job of improving the performance of public enterprises.

Overall, the welfare consequences were positive. There were large gains to buyers in all cases. There were some smaller gains to government. Workers overall came out as winners, largely because they were able to buy shares of their companies at low prices—and did so—and because those who were laid off got generous severance payments.

These three cases confirm the reputation of the United Kingdom as a pacesetter in privatization.

Comments

John Moore

The researchers on the U.K. cases argue that the Conservative government had two principal objectives for its divestiture program: denationalization and liberalization. I disagree. From my experience preparing a comprehensive thesis on privatization for the government, it is perfectly clear that there was one straightforward, absolute goal: denationalization, an end to state ownership. Liberalization may have been a necessary consequence of transferring de facto monopolies from public to private control, but it was not the primary objective.

The researchers also state that the government wanted to encourage wider share ownership, partly to make it difficult for any future government to renationalize. This is, of course, a perfectly proper and practical objective of the government, and it did play a role. But having said that, I think the case studies miss an important point: the fundamental desire on the part of so many who had no experience with share ownership to secure all the benefits that come from a genuine diffusion of ownership. I do not think you can understand the British experience unless you understand the passion that we created for ownership, and the impact it has had on our people.

The researchers further suggest that the goal of fostering wide ownership may have been in conflict with the goal of promoting efficiency. There is no question that diffused, massive share ownership is more comfortable for management. But in the modern world—and I speak as an investment banker now—people underestimate the pressure of rational capital markets, the pressure of analysts, the pressure of institutions for efficiency. It is my view from many years of experience in the financial world that widespread diffuse ownership does not lead to management laxity or prevent proper strategic decisionmaking. I think some research work ought to be done in this area.

There are three main issues with which I would argue, and I will limit myself largely to the British Telecom case. The first relates to the capital constraints, the second to productivity changes, and the third to whether—and how much—additional welfare has been created.

The researchers argue that the capital constraint would not have been maintained beyond 1987 under continued public operation. They assume that as deteriorating services led to public outcry and the government's fiscal situation improved, investment would increase. As a former government minister with ten years of experience with government decisionmaking on capital expenditure, I fundamentally and profoundly disagree. The case assumes that, yes, there was a radical increase in investment after divestiture, but that the difference between the privatized British Telecom and the counterfactual public British Telecom will ultimately disappear, that the pattern of constrained investment typical of the public British Telecom in the 1960s and 1970s would actually change. I think that is utterly wrong. The public is not out there vociferously demanding more spending on the latest developments in the telephone industry. Public pressures on governments will always be for more spending on hospitals, roads, schools—the traditional areas of government concern.

To support their argument, the researchers point to increases in public spending on railways and electricity since divestiture. That is certainly true, but the spending was very limited, very specifically directed to the repair of the ravages of the past. I was transport secretary when we increased spending on the railways, and I do not think that increased public investment spending can be taken as a long-term assumption. Look at what happened to proposals to mend some of the sewer problems in the preprivatized water industry. All the proposed investments had rates of return far above any that a normal private sector entity would expect, and yet none could meet the limited criteria for finance with state money.

Similarly, the researchers doubt that British Telecom's productivity improvement can be linked to institutional change. But consider the enormous increments to fixed capital—in constant prices—the differences between an average annual growth of 4.7 percent before divestiture and 7.4 percent after. Any heavily capital-intensive entity requires capital investments to improve its productivity. Consider also that even the case study finds that progress was made in "adapting the work force to changed practices in the telecommunication industry, something that British Telecom was unable to achieve before divestiture." The ability to change working practices, albeit slowly since you are dealing with huge monoliths of 200,000 plus people, is an important outcome of privatization. Further, even an examination of the case study's own data on productivity change—number of lines, personnel, and inland calls—suggests a greater change after divestiture than the study is willing to credit. Ignore for the moment what we have all noticed, the increased number of phone boxes now available and actually working and the ability to get equipment repaired almost immediately, and look instead at the growth in the number of inland calls. From 1979 to 1984, the Deutsche Bundesposte increased the total number of inland calls by 36.4 percent, British Telecom by 23.4 percent. After privatization, British Telecom's record surpassed that of Deutsche Bundesposte: British Telecom's inland calls rose by 50 percent, Deutsche Bundesposte's by 19 percent.

Finally, the case study states quite clearly that "the bulk of the increase [in welfare] was due to an exogenous tax increase." Since I was the financial secretary who changed the tax system in 1984, I have some notion of what we were doing. We radically changed the tax system, but that does not affect the fact that extra wealth was created as a consequence of British Telecom's divestiture; it affects only the distribution of that wealth.

The case study rightly points to the difficulties of privatizing large monopolies. Nevertheless, my final message to any ministry seeking to privatize is to do the big utilities first, whether they are profitable or unprofitable. However difficult, privatizing the large utilities will ultimately have a much more profound impact on the overall economy than the easier privatizing of competitive firms.

David Newbery

The choice of cases for the United Kingdom is interesting. They cover a wide range, from British Telecom, a natural monopoly, to British Airways, an oligopoly in the domestic market but facing competition in international markets, and National Freight, operating in the competitive domestic market.

At first glance it might appear that the privatizing of National Freight should go well because there are no problems of market power. Yet this is the one U.K. case in which the government lost. As a result, the Treasury seems to have overreacted, becoming so worried about management buy-outs that it now puts enormous resources into making sure that the Treasury does not lose. In the recent privatization of British Technology Group, the cost of hiring experts and lawyers was as much as half the value of the final sale.

As for natural monopolies, the studies for all four countries make very clear the critical role of the regulatory regime. For the United Kingdom, regulation is an important issue not only in the case of British Telecom. When British Gas was sold, it was the lone supplier to the domestic sector. Only gradually has it come to face competition. The water companies are also monopolies in the areas they serve, as is the electricity distribution system. All these are natural monopolies, and all are subject to a regulatory regime that has interesting, innovative features.

The difficulty of reconciling opposing interests when setting up a regulatory regime should not be underestimated. On the one hand, the objective of consumers and economists concerned with social welfare is that prices be kept at competitive, efficient levels. On the other hand, potential investors have to be confident that they will be able to enjoy the profits of their investments and that they will make enough profits on the investments that are successful to offset those that are not.

This conflict or potential conflict between these two interests can be resolved in various ways. The U.S. cost-plus system of regulation is good for reassuring investors that they will enjoy a reasonable return no matter what they invest. The problem, of course, is that it encourages them to overinvest and does not provide incentives for cost cutting. So the innovation in the United Kingdom was the RPI minus x formula, which has good incentive properties if investors believe that the x will be objectively set. In British Telecom's history, there have been three values of x: an initial 3 percent, which was rather generous since the Treasury always thought that British Telecom ought to be able to achieve 5.00 percent productivity growth, followed by 4.50 percent and, eventually, but with a wider basket of goods, including immensely profitable foreign calls, 6.25 percent.

The worry facing those who are risking a durable and expensive investment is that once they have restructured the industry and put in the new capital, the regulators might turn around and increase the x factor and take away the profits. A critical and not adequately recognized achievement of the British privatization program is the widespread confidence in the independence and proper functioning of the regulatory process. The regulator has an interest in convincing the industry that it is not there to expropriate its profits but to protect consumers. Achieving that balance is an intrinsically difficult task, and one should note that achievement in the United Kingdom.

The times have also been very favorable to the success of privatization. In the electricity industry, for instance, combined-cycle gas turbines became available around the time of privatization, providing a cheap, quickly constructed, and efficient means of generating electricity. The risks of investment fell dramatically compared to the time when nuclear power seemed to be the future of energy and when construction periods were long, investments durable, and capital costs enormous. Now if the world changes again, and nuclear investment needs to be reconsidered, would that be feasible in a privatized and regulated system? Only if people have confidence in the independence, objectivity, and efficiency orientation of the regulators. But creating that reputation is not an easy task.

What are the failures or the disappointments of the British system? I think the single greatest failure is the continuing lack of competition in some of these privatized industries. One can debate how much competition might reasonably have been introduced into the telecommunications industry. My discussion with the regulators in the British Telecom case suggests that the objective was to encourage the maximum amount of competition possible without excessive duplication. There is always the problem with a natural monopoly that encouraging competition will lead to a substantial increase in total cost. So the benefits to be derived from increased competition—and they are very real—need to be weighed against the extra cost of duplicate investments.

If I have one criticism of the methodology, it is a very small one, and that is that the counterfactual does not include the alternative of keeping a company in the public sector and restructuring or introducing other changes before selling it under a different format. As long as a company remains in the public sector the options remain open. As soon as an enterprise is sold, the options are foreclosed.

However, what must be weighed against the foreclosed options are the benefits of selling, especially the benefits of learning more about how to do it well.

Finally, one of the exciting things we have discovered is just what a powerful mechanism the market is for revealing information. When the electricity industry was privatized, we discovered in the case of a nuclear power station now nearing completion that the figures churned out by the enormously time-consuming and expensive investigative inquiry were completely bogus and that, essentially, £50 million of taxpayers' money for a select committee to look into the matter had been seriously misapplied. There is nothing like the test of the market to expose shaky arguments.

6

CHILE

Ahmed Galal

In reporting on the findings and analysis for the three divestiture cases in Chile, I will emphasize two questions: Has divestiture benefited Chile, and how may other countries benefit from Chile's experience? What I hope to convey clearly is that divestiture is an equal opportunity reform: it benefits developing countries as well as industrialized countries like the United Kingdom. Indeed, I would even argue that Chile's experience is in many ways more profound than that of the United Kingdom, thanks, in particular, to its innovative approach to regulation, especially in the power sector.

How Important Is Chile's Divestiture Program?

Professor Paul Sigmund of Princeton University described the privatization experience of Chile saying, "In no country in the world, not even in Margaret Thatcher's Britain, has privatization been carried out as far as it has in contemporary Chile." Sigmund is right for at least three reasons.

First, Chile reduced the size of the public enterprise sector from 39 percent of GDP in 1973 to 16 percent in 1989—or to 6.6 percent if the state-owned copper mine, the largest in the world, is taken out of the calculation. Along with this dramatic decline in the size of the public enterprise sector has come a dramatic decline in the role of the state.

Second, Chile's divestiture program is extensive, covering not only enterprises in competitive sectors producing tradable goods like steel, textiles, fertilizer, and sugar, but also enterprises in monopolistic markets, such as electricity and telephone companies.

Third, Chile has consistently pursued its divestiture program within the context of macroeconomic reform in general and public enterprise reform in particular. Starting in 1974, the government worked aggressively to liberalize foreign trade. It eliminated all trade restrictions in one shot and set uniform tariffs at 10 percent across the board. On the public enterprise front, Chile introduced significant reforms to boost the efficiency of public enterprises before they were privatized. Thus in the Chilean case studies we were able to examine whether divestiture of relatively efficient enterprises benefits the economy.

Chile did not privatize overnight, nor has its privatization experience been without pitfalls. The first divestiture episode of the 1970s led to a concentration of ownership in some cases and to bankruptcy for some enterprises during the recession of the early 1980s and takeover by the government. The cases reviewed here, however, are from a later and more successful wave of privatizations in the second half of the 1980s.

What Happened to Performance in Divested Firms?

The three cases examined here include two in the electricity sector and one in telecommunications. The first case is Chilgener, one of eleven electricity-generating companies connected to Chile's main electrical grid. The second is Enersis, the sole electricity distribution company in the Santiago metropolitan area. The third is Chile Telecom, which provides 95 percent of local telecommunication services (most long-distance service is provided by another company, ENTEL).

Three key indicators are useful for comparing the performance of these companies before and after privatization: private profitability, which measures the bottom line for private shareholders; total factor productivity, which removes price effects to show what happens to productivity; and investment, which shows the dynamic effect of divestiture over a longer period of time (figure 6.1).

Private profitability improved in all three firms after privatization. It improved sharply in Enersis, substantially in Chile Telecom, and less dramatically in Chilgener.

Figure 6.1 Chile: Changes in Key Indicators

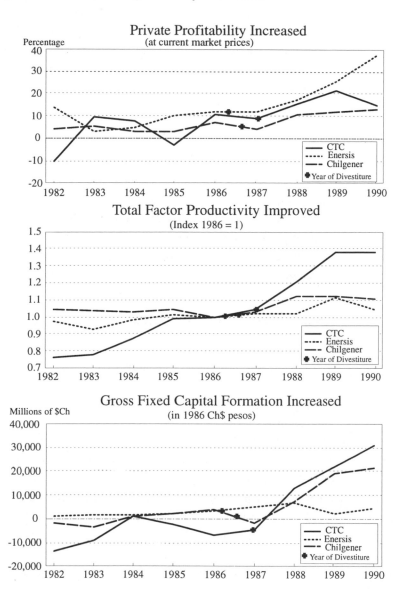

Source: Galal Ahmed, with contributions from Raul Saez and Clemencia Torres, "Chile," in Ahmed Galal, Leroy Jones, Pankaj Tandon, and Ingo Vogelsang, *Welfare Consequences of Selling Public Enterprises: Case Studies from Chile, Malaysia, Mexico and the United Kingdom* (New York: Oxford University Press, forthcoming).

Profitability is influenced by prices as well as by quantities. Getting rid of the price effect lets us derive a measure of productivity. Total factor productivity essentially measures the index of the quantity of output to the index of the quantity of inputs. The results are similar to those for profitability: Chile Telecom improved dramatically, Chilgener more modestly, and Enersis more modestly still.

Fixed capital formation also rose after privatization, particularly in the case of Chile Telecom. Following privatization in 1988, the company increased the number of lines in service in the next four years by 72 percent, the largest increase in the company's history. That kind of change is going to make a difference in any bottom line. The expansion illustrates the argument that privatization, by relaxing the investment constraint, can make a tremendous difference for an infrastructure company like Chile Telecom.

We find, then, that performance improved after privatization in all three companies as measured by all three indicators. The differences are of degree only, not kind.

Would the Changes Have Taken Place without Divestiture?

Looking only at what happened isn't enough to say that divestiture benefits society. To determine how much of the change is due to privatization requires looking at what would have happened without privatization—the counterfactual.

I said earlier that changes can come from prices, productivity, or investment. Divestiture did not actually change prices in the case of Chilgener or Chile Telecom, because both firms had been regulated since 1982, well before their privatization. Even as public enterprises, the companies operated under the kind of regulatory regime usually applied to privately owned firms. This is a unique feature of the Chilean cases. An independent regulatory body was created for the energy sector in 1978, and the same rules have applied to public and private firms since then.

While the changes in prices were not due to divestiture in the cases of Chilgener or Chile Telecom, they were due to divestiture in the case of Enersis. Why?

After privatization, Enersis reduced electricity theft or losses from something like 21 percent to 15 percent in 1989, a dramatic change. Under the Chilean regulation system, a reduction in losses means that in the next round regulators will allow less return to the company. So the company makes some extra money at first, but later the regulators capture those gains and translate them into lower tariffs for all paying consumers. The result is a more efficient reallocation of resources in which a few consumers lose, but more of them gain.

By contrast, divestiture was responsible for the productivity improvement in the cases of Chilgener and Chile Telecom, but not in the case of Enersis. Let's focus on the exception again. Although it is true that productivity in Enersis improved after divestiture, it is also true that productivity moved in parallel with growth in the economy. As GDP grows, so does demand for electricity, so the company is able to sell more and use more of its existing capacity. Productivity improves simply because demand is increasing. Since privatization does not boost demand, that change in productivity was not attributed to privatization.

Investment rose in all three companies, but in Chilgener and Enersis, the increase was not due to privatization since the two companies grew pretty much according to their trend growth rates. Chile Telecom's case is different. For one thing, the industry was facing excess demand. For another, the government sold part of the company to foreign investors by selling new shares and expanding the size of the company. Chile Telecom is a very different company now from what it was before privatization. It is nearly twice as large as before, and given its current investment plans, the company is likely to grow even faster in the next five years.

Thus not all the changes that accompanied divestiture were due to divestiture. Those that were included reduced tariffs in the case of Enersis, improved productivity in the cases of Chilgener and Chile Telecom, and increased investment in the case of Chile Telecom. What differences do these changes make in the bottom line?

What Is the Bottom Line?

Two points stand out. The first is that divestitures made both Chile and the world better off than before. The second is that the gains were dramatically larger for Chile Telecom than for the other two companies. The difference is accounted for primarily by the fact that Chilgener and Enersis were relatively well run before divestiture. The gains in cases of that kind are relatively modest, though important nonetheless. But for Chile Telecom, relaxation of the investment constraint brought about significant welfare gains not only for Chile, but for the world—gains larger than in any other of the case studies.

Where did the gains come from? For Chilgener, the gains came from a modest improvement in productivity (figure 6.2), for Enersis from output diversification and price change. The price change, as mentioned, came about through a reduction in theft and led to a reallocation of consumption. Output diversification was part of a package of changes through which Enersis used existing facilities, created subsidiaries, and capitalized on economies of scope by selling equipment as well as distributing electricity. For Chile Telecom, the biggest change was in investment, with some modest changes in productivity and output diversification into value-added services, such as cellular phone and data transmission services.

Almost every group came out ahead as a result of the divestitures (figure 6.3). Buyers, including workers as shareholders, were better off. Consumers were better off because of the expansion and better services. Foreigners were better off, but so were nationals. The only negatives were the slight government losses in the sales of Chilgener and Enersis. This result poses an interesting question. What should happen in a case where the government loses but everybody else wins? Should the privatization go ahead? From a public welfare perspective the answer is yes, the divestiture should take place even if the government loses in the long run.

Conclusion

Several important lessons emerge from Chile's divestiture experience. One is that the process matters. While this presentation touches only briefly on this point, the more detailed case studies show that when governments don't pay attention to what they are selling, whom they are selling it to, and how, they can get into trouble. Chile's early experience with divestiture shows just what can happen when the details are neglected. The government had to take over some

Figure 6.2 Chile: Origins of Change in Welfare

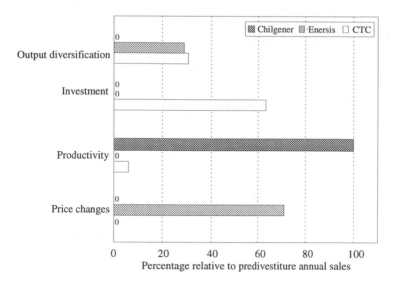

Figure 6.3 Chile: Who Won? Who Lost?

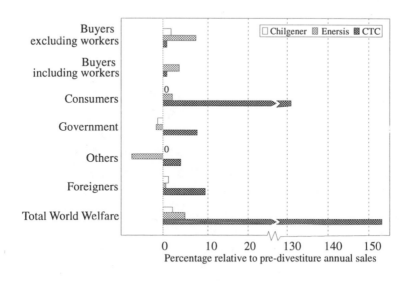

Source: Galal Ahmed, with contributions from Raul Saez and Clemencia Torres, "Chile," in Ahmed Galal, Leroy Jones, Pankaj Tandon, and Ingo Vogelsang, *Welfare Consequences of Selling Public Enterprises: Case Studies from Chile, Malaysia, Mexico and the United Kingdom* (N ew York: Oxford University Press, forthcoming).

enterprises that went bankrupt, primarily because it did not pay enough attention to how the financing took place. Some buyers used one company as collateral to buy another.

A second lesson is that regulation is critical. Some people would argue that little is lost by not regulating—just a little triangle of allocative inefficiency. The real problem, however, is that it's not just a question of allocative efficiency, but of income distribution as well. If government doesn't regulate, monopolies can exploit consumers. And the transfer from consumers to producers can be a big one, which makes it worth worrying about.

A third lesson is that divestiture can mobilize resources. That is most evident in the Chile Telecom case. There was pent up demand for telecommunications and a need for expansion, but the government did not have the resources to make the necessary investments. Divestiture brought in a significant flow of capital, to the great benefit of society.

The fourth and last point is that if you have a case for divestiture in which all groups will win, but at some fiscal cost to the government, the deal is still worth pursuing.

Comments

Jorge Marshall

This is groundbreaking research, particularly in its focus on the microeconomic effects of divestiture on welfare. I will consider primarily the welfare issues.

Except for Chile Telecom, the welfare improvements in the three Chilean cases were modest. That raises an interesting issue. Important reforms were instituted in the state enterprise sector before privatization, including precise definition of profitability and efficiency objectives, elimination of preferential treatment, implementation of a realistic pricing scheme, establishment of strict self-financing criteria, and cutbacks in employment. These reforms left less room for improvement in efficiency after divestiture than is usually the case for public enterprises in developing countries. Thus privatizations in other developing countries are likely to yield even greater welfare gains than those of Chile.

Large welfare gains in the case of Chile Telecom were attributed to the lifting of the investment constraint following privatization. I tend to agree with that interpretation. There was considerable scope for economies of scale in Chile Telecom that went unfulfilled because of underinvestment: I really don't see the government of Chile making the kind of investment in telecommunications that its private owners made. I am in that government now and I think there is very little chance that we could undertake a large program of investment in telecommunications, considering our other priorities. I am convinced that privatization was the only way to reduce the gap between demand and supply in the telecommunications sector. (It is an interesting side note that Chile Telecom is the only case on which the government and the buyer agreed in advance on an investment program.)

I have some problems with the counterfactual analysis for Chile Telecom. The simulations show a gap between the outcomes for the privatized Chile Telecom and those for a Chile Telecom that remains in the public sector. Changing some of the assumptions would reduce that gap. For example, much of the gain under privatization comes from a realization of economies of scale, yet the simulation assumes constant returns to scale. The assumption of a constant number of calls per line is also questionable. And the state enterprise in the simulation exercise starts at a lower level than the privatized enterprise, with less capacity and fewer lines. The assumption about residential versus commercial service is also problematic, since commercial service is less restrictive in terms of rationing in any market than is residential service. Changing these assumptions would not necessarily wipe out the gap, but it would reduce it.

I have a few comments about the other two cases as well, but primarily about Enersis. First, Enersis is not the company that was sold. Chilmetro was. The government sold an electricity distribution company called Chilmetro, and that company is now part of Enersis, a conglomerate of five companies, two of them electricity distribution companies and three of them production companies functioning in competitive sectors. So shouldn't this diversification be viewed as the result of the investment strategy of the conglomerate rather than that of the electricity distribution company? That difference is something the methodology ought to take into account.

My last point on Enersis concerns the effect of losses from theft. Sixty percent of the welfare gain from privatizing Enersis is attributed to reduced losses from theft. I agree that the losses were important, but I disagree about their origin. There is a relationship between the losses of the electricity company and the general condition of the economy. When unemployment is at 25 percent, losses rise not only in electricity distribution firms but in other public utilities as well. When the economy recovers, losses shrink across the board. Indeed, as the economy recovered, losses fell among water supply companies as well, even though none had been privatized. So some of the improvement in Enersis is due to external factors, not to privatization.

One final point. While I agree that the regulatory scheme is important, I would also point out that privatization creates an opportunity to define a new market structure by opening up space to introduce more competition. Market competition always works better than regulatory authorities. For that reason, we are now trying to introduce more competition into the electricity sector by separating the distribution, transmission, and generation functions. We are trying to do the same thing in telecommunications.

To conclude, I agree in the main with the findings of the Chilean case studies. The gains from privatization of the electricity companies were not as impressive as those for the telecommunications company because much of the gain had already been realized through earlier reform of the state enterprises. The gains in the case of Chile Telecom are important, and they would not have occurred without privatization. Finally, regulation—if we think of it as the way the government goes about setting prices—is not enough, especially where institutions are weak. Introducing more competition, even if that means incurring some costs in terms of market failure, is better than regulatory failure.

Rolf Luders

I believe that this research marks a turning point in the empirical work on privatization. Till now, most of us have worked on the partial effects of privatization on this or that variable. A lot of theoretical work has been done, but I know of no attempt before this one to actually measure the welfare gains or losses of privatization. I cannot stress enough what an important breakthrough this is. I also believe that the methodology used is the right one, although it can be improved in many ways.

I agree with the conclusions of the three Chilean case studies—and with those of the overall study. Two findings stand out. One is that in all three cases the welfare gains were positive. The other is that regulation was very important.

An interesting point about the Chilean cases is the government losses in two of the privatizations. I agree with Ahmed Galal that it really doesn't matter; what matters is what happens to the country's welfare.

Another interesting aspect of the cases is the tremendous insight brought out by the counterfactual analyses, which make the studies very rich. It is also the case, however, that the methodology is speculative. Once you start talking about the counterfactual and projecting your findings, you are necessarily involved in speculation. One way to improve on that might be to use probability distributions for the different variables that are being projected, as is commonly done in project evaluation work. That would give a kind of probability distribution of the welfare gains for the country or the world or for each group instead of simply a point estimate of the end result. That would also help to avoid one of the dangers of this sort of this methodology, which is the tendency to treat all these generated numbers as though they were true. Using probability distributions makes it much clearer that the numbers are estimates.

In the Chilean cases the differences between the market prices of shares and the discounted private value of the cash flows in 1990 and in 1986 or 1987, or in whatever year the privatizations took place, seems to have puzzled some people. The differences are very small around 1990, but they are huge around 1987.

There are many reasons such differences might arise. The case study attributes the differences to risk-averse small investors. Given their limited resources, it doesn't make economic sense for them to do much investigation before they invest, so to compensate they are willing to pay less for their shares than a larger investor would. So market shares are worth less than the discounted value of the cash flows. I don't believe that is true in the Chilean case, however, because huge pension funds bought and traded most of these shares on the stock exchange, and these funds certainly have people who routinely conduct thorough investigations. Other explanations are that the capital market was imperfect or that there was fraud of some sort. Well, I don't buy those explanations either, since by 1986 the stock market in Chile was functioning relatively well.

I think the answer lies elsewhere. As I understand it, cash flows in the study are arbitrarily discounted by 10 percent—that was the discount rate selected. Well, the fact is that if the capital asset pricing model is used instead to estimate a discount rate—as we did in our book—the discount rates are much higher than 10 percent in the initial years around 1985-87 and just about 10 percent for recent years, which immediately solves the puzzle of why there are such big differences in the early years that nearly disappear around 1990.

If this explanation is right, then the government actually sold the enterprises at their true worth in 1986 and 1987. With the discount rates that were relevant in those years, the prices more or less reflected the true value of the companies. My guess is that applying the right discount rate will show that the government would have lost very little. The losses probably don't disappear entirely because the government sold shares at subsidized prices to workers, but they will be much smaller.

Finally, with respect to the telephone company, I believe that had Chile Telecom remained in government hands, the government would have invested substantial resources in expanding the telephone system—perhaps not as much as private investors spent, but a substantial amount nonetheless. The history of the industry before 1970 shows that the government has always been willing to put money into the country's telephone system.

7

MEXICO

Pankaj Tandon

Mexico privatized on a large scale, as part of a far-reaching economic reform program. One of Mexico's key goals for privatization was to raise revenue and ease some of the fiscal problems of the government. Liberalization, deregulation, and efficiency enhancement were also important goals, but in my opinion they were subsidiary. Revenue was the primary motive.

The number of public enterprises shrank from 1,155 in 1982 to about 200 today. Thus our three case studies, the telephone monopoly Telmex and the two major airlines Aeromexico and Mexicana Airlines, are only three of many. Revenues from privatization have totaled more than $15 billion in the past ten years, more than double the revenues from privatization of any other developing country in the same period (figure 7.1).

The privatization proceeds compare very favorably to the savings in capital outflows since the Brady Agreement took effect in July 1989. Since then, Mexico has saved an estimated $1.3 billion a year in interest payments. If the reduced principal payments resulting from the lengthening maturity of the debt structure are taken into account as well, Mexico saved an estimated $4 billion a year in capital outflow. In 1990 and 1991, the last two years for which we have data, privatization proceeds have totaled $14 billion. So actually this program has been more significant in this period than the debt rescheduling.

Let me turn now to the cases.

Figure 7.1 Mexico: Sales Revenues from Privatization

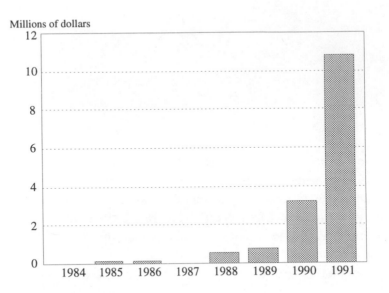

Source: Tandon, Pankaj, with contributions from Manuel Abdala and Inder Ruprah, "Mexico," in Ahmed Galal, Leroy Jones, Pankaj Tandon, and Ingo Vogelsang, *Welfare Consequences of Selling Public Enterprises: Case Studies from Chile, Malaysia, Mexico and the United Kingdom* (New York: Oxford University Press, forthcoming).

Mexicana Airline

Mexicana Airline had about 13,500 workers and a fleet of about 50 aircraft when it was privatized. The government had twice before tried, unsuccessfully, to sell it. In 1989 the company was finally sold to a group that contributed $140 million in new equity in exchange for a 20 percent ownership share. The government received no revenue from the sale of Mexicana, since the money was put into the airline as an equity infusion, and the government's ownership share was diluted from about 52 percent to 40 percent. The buyers were also required to purchase an additional 5 percent of Mexicana stock on the open market. The government placed 25 percent of its shares into a trust, giving the buying group voting control over the company. The buying group also has an option to buy the shares in this trust at the same implicit price that it paid for the original equity holding.

The new buyers began a massive investment program, putting $1.6 billion into the company over a period of a few years. The plan was to completely refurbish and modernize the Mexicana fleet. They placed orders for twenty-two new Airbus aircraft and have options on fourteen more. In most cases, the relaxation of the investment constraint thanks to privatization improves welfare, since there are very profitable or socially desirable investments that a public company cannot make because the government lacks the funds. In the case of Mexicana, however, the investment program turned out to be disastrous. Its timing was bad, coming as it did just when the world airline market went into a prolonged slump. As a result, Mexicana is an exceptional case in which relaxation of the investment constraint reduced welfare.

The buyers made other mistakes as well. Because one of the buyers had resort interests, the airline concentrated on tourist traffic. But the worldwide recession and the Persian Gulf war took a heavy toll on this traffic. The new management also tried to sell tours to the Mexican resorts directly rather than through the well-established network of agents in the United States, another mistake. Aggressive expansion into new routes and the addition of more flights on existing routes also proved to be miscalculations. The mistakes are reflected in the stock market: the market value of Mexicana is now about $200 million, far less than its implicit value of $700 million at the time the airline was sold. Another mistake—one that is nearly always mentioned in discussions of the airline—was the decision to repaint the aircraft. At a cost of $32 million, not only was the painting itself expensive, but the added weight reduced the fuel economy of the aircraft.

Not all the news about Mexicana Airline has been bad, however (figure 7.2). The work force shrank by 20 percent, although the slim down began in 1988, before privatization. Productivity rose some 12 percent, but labor morale fell, and relations with labor unions have been poor.

Figure 7.2 Mexicana: Sources of Net Gain

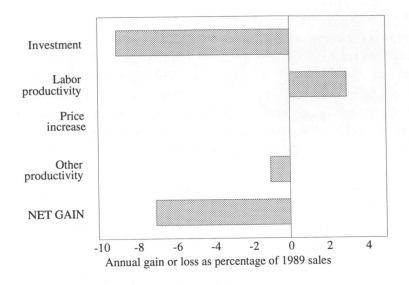

Figure 7.3 Mexicana: Who Won? Who Lost?

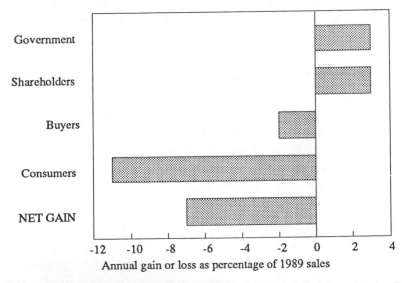

Source: Tandon, Pankaj, with contributions from Manuel Abdala and Inder Ruprah, "Mexico," in Ahmed Galal, Leroy Jones, Pankaj Tandon, and Ingo Vogelsang, *Welfare Consequences of Selling Public Enterprises: Case Studies from Chile, Malaysia, Mexico and the United Kingdom* (New York: Oxford University Press, forthcoming).

So who won and who lost? The government and the original private shareholders both gained a little—an indication that the airline would have been less profitable without the privatization, primarily because of the low domestic prices (figure 7.3).

The new shareholders are losers, even taking into account that deregulation, which I view as part of the privatization process, will allow domestic prices to rise. The buyers paid too much for the airline and, as a result, are slight losers. Consumers also lose because of the higher domestic prices. The bottom line is that privatization can turn out poorly if the buyers make too many bad decisions. Private companies don't always perform well.

Aeromexico

I won't discuss the entire Aeromexico case, but will only point out that it is interesting because it was bankrupted before sale. The airline had had only three profitable years over the last thirty years, and the government thought it would be unable to sell this money-loser. But when the union went on a strike in early 1988, the government seized the opportunity and declared the company bankrupt, terminated all labor contracts, and sold the company's assets.

What has been the outcome of the privatization? Aeromexico no longer receives government subsidies, and productivity rose by about 24 percent (figure 7.4). (The labor force went from 11,500 to 6,500).

Who won and who lost? The government was the big gainer (figure 7.5), primarily through the elimination of subsidies, and the shareholders also gained to some extent. The losers are the creditors at the time Aeromexico was declared bankrupt. Many creditors have already accepted 70 cents on the dollar. Creditors who are holding out will have to accept what the bankruptcy court decides for them, but our calculations show that government will not be able to discharge all its liabilities, so they are unlikely to do any better.

The other losers are consumers because prices have gone up. The rise in prices should not be seen as bad, however. The previous regulated prices were uneconomically low, and in fact welfare is now rising as a result of the price changes. Workers are not actually much worse off than before because those that were laid off were given generous severance allowances of about one year's pay.

Figure 7.4 Aeromexico: Sources of Net Gain

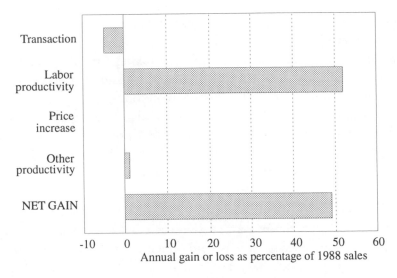

Annual gain or loss as percentage of 1988 sales

Figure 7.5 Aeromexico: Who Won? Who Lost?

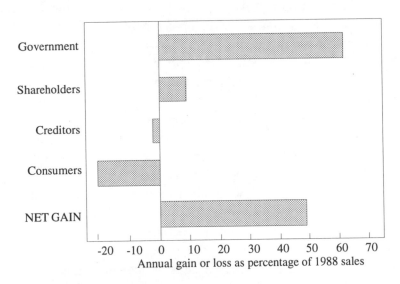

Annual gain or loss as percentage of 1988 sales

Source: Tandon, Pankaj, with contributions from Manuel Abdala and Inder Ruprah, "Mexico," in Ahmed Galal, Leroy Jones, Pankaj Tandon, and Ingo Vogelsang, *Welfare Consequences of Selling Public Enterprises: Case Studies from Chile, Malaysia, Mexico and the United Kingdom* (New York: Oxford University Press, forthcoming).

Telmex

Telefonos de Mexico, or Telmex, had some 50,000 to 60,000 workers when privatized in 1990. It had been nationalized in 1972, but it continued to have partial private ownership and was quoted on the stock exchange. At the time of privatization the government's share was 55 percent.

Since Telmex's nationalization, telephone services had been taxed at high and slightly increasing rates (on a pre-profit basis) to generate stable revenues for the government. Thus the government received revenue from the company through taxes rather than by virtue of its share ownership. Telmex remained marginally profitable throughout this period, and even declared a slight dividend each year, but service was very poor.

In 1988, well before Telmex's privatization, the Mexican government embarked on a major investment program to expand and modernize the telephone system. While this large investment program continued after privatization, it is not attributed to the privatization, which it clearly predated. When the decision was made to privatize Telmex in 1990, the company was considered too large to sell in one shot, given the size of Mexico's capital market. The government came up with an inventive solution that changed the capital structure of the company.

A dividend of one-and-a-half shares was declared for each share of existing stock. What made the change innovative was that the newly issued shares had no voting rights or very limited ones. That meant that voting rights were vested in 40 percent of the shares. The government then offered half of those shares, or some 20 percent of the company, for sale. But this 20 percent of the company had 51 percent of the voting rights. The government was able to sell just 20 percent of the company and yet guarantee the buyers voting control of the company.

The winning bid was submitted by a consortium led by a Mexican conglomerate, which owned 51 percent of the buying group. The other 49 percent was split between Southwestern Bell and France Telecom. The government wanted some foreign ownership for the technological know-how that would come with it. The winning bid from the consortium for 20 percent of the company was $1.75 billion. The implicit value of Telmex at the time of the sale was therefore roughly $8 billion. Six months later, in May 1991, the government placed an additional 15 percent of the stock on the international stock market (the company is now quoted on the New York Stock Exchange). The stocks went for a price that implied a value for the company as a whole of $15 billion. So Telmex had approximately doubled in value in just six months.

Several other changes affected Telmex, key among them the price reform that took place just before privatization. Prices for domestic telephone services had been kept very low for years, while international calls were expensive by world standards. The price reform involved a major rebalancing that lowered international prices and boosted domestic prices dramatically. The change was not made all at once, however, and the process is a continuing one.

At about the same time, the telephone tax was abolished, making the company much more attractive to buyers. A new regulatory mechanism, a price cap similar to that applied in the case of British Telecom, was announced and introduced simultaneously with the divestiture. For the first few years after privatization, the average price of telephone services was permitted to rise at the rate of price inflation.

In addition to the price regulation, the government introduced minimum investment and network expansion standards. The network must be expanded by at least 12 percent a year until 1996. Some requirements for quality were also established, such as acceptable response times on repairs. Competition was also introduced in certain areas, such as private circuits and yellow pages.

To win over employees to the privatization, the government offered them loans from a government bank to enable them to purchase 4.4 percent of the stock for $325 million. The bank now holds the shares in trust to ensure payment of the loan. The strategy seems to have worked: employees have benefited to the tune of some $1 billion in increased share value.

The Telmex privatization is still too recent for the effects to be readily measured but some effects have been quite strong. Total factor productivity in 1991 was 15 percent higher than before privatization. The stock price of Telmex quadrupled in one year, which reveals the

Figure 7.6 Telmex: Sources of Net Gain

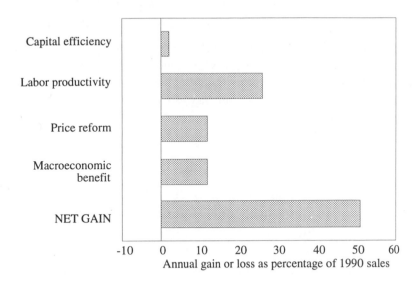

Figure 7.7 Telmex: Who Won? Who Lost?

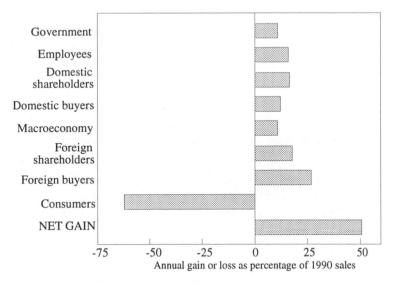

Source: Tandon, Pankaj, with contributions from Manuel Abdala and Inder Ruprah, "Mexico," in Ahmed Galal, Leroy Jones, Pankaj Tandon, and Ingo Vogelsang, *Welfare Consequences of Selling Public Enterprises: Case Studies from Chile, Malaysia, Mexico and the United Kingdom* (New York: Oxford University Press, forthcoming).

market's assessment of privatization. The bottom line is a net gain of 51 percent of the annuity value of 1991 sales (figure 7.6).

Who won and who lost? The gains are pretty well spread out (figure 7.7). The government gained. It continues to be a shareholder, so the value of its shares rises with the value of the company. Interestingly, the increased income taxes from Telmex are likely to compensate for the lost revenue from the telephone tax. In addition to government, other winners were employees, domestic shareholders, and buyers, both domestic and foreign. Foreign buyers have gained 27 percent of 1991 sales, so there has been substantial leakage of benefits abroad. There were gains to the macroeconomy as well, as a result of the large capital infusion the government received from the sale. I believe that infusion made an important contribution to Mexico's recent macroeconomic stability.

Consumers were the only losers. They lost mainly because of the price increases. It is important to emphasize, however, that this welfare loss to consumers is not net of any gain from improved quality, which could be substantial. The biggest price changes have been in connection charges and the cost of measured local calls, which rose sixfold. The price reform has improved welfare, an indication that the previous prices were not welfare optimal. So even though consumers have lost, the gains to the firm outweigh the losses to consumers, resulting in the net positive effect.

Lessons

What lessons can be derived from the Mexican case studies? First, divestiture can raise large amounts of revenue to help stabilize the economy. While many people have been skeptical that this could be done, Mexico shows otherwise.

Second, the contrasting examples of Aeromexico and Mexicana Airline suggest that if it is possible to restructure staffing before divestiture, there are gains from doing so. Mexicana Airline has been unable to reach agreement with its unions on scaling back employment. Aeromexico, because it passed through bankruptcy first, was able to hire only the workers it needed.

Third, divestiture can lead to welfare-improving price reform. Here, we find that privatization was accompanied by a loosening of price regulation and a movement toward market-determined welfare-optimal prices.

A fourth lesson is that if government decides to sell cheap, it shouldn't sell to foreigners. The quadrupling of the market price in one year strongly suggests that the initial price of Telmex shares was too low. If the government wants to keep share prices low to encourage broad ownership, it would do better not to sell such a large proportion of shares to foreigners.

Finally, it is possible to sell loss-making companies successfully. Governments tend to target the good-looking companies, but economic theory—and the Aeromexico case—tell us that a loss-making company can be sold if the price is right.

Comments

Manuel Sanchez

The Mexican case studies have interesting policy implications for divestitures in Mexico and elsewhere. While I believe that the methodology is fundamentally sound, I disagree with some of the results and interpretations.

The researchers offer multiple—sometimes confusing—indicators of the performance of the firms before and after divestiture. While mixed results are a common characteristic of empirical studies in economics, I think that too much emphasis on calculations weakens the analyses and conclusions of this study.

Why did the changes happen? The researchers attribute to divestiture the set of economic policies that happened to coincide with the selling of a public enterprise. Thus in the case of Telmex, the researchers recognize that the upward turn in total factor productivity after 1989 can be partly explained by the sharp drop in the capital share as interest and inflation rates fell. Yet they later conclude that "productivity has been improving since divestiture" as though divestiture played a causal role, when they had already rightly assigned that role to the macroeconomy (inflation and interest rates). In the Aeromexico case, the researchers state that a dramatic effect accompanying divestiture has been the sharp drop in output. Yet declining output is an obvious consequence of any bankruptcy and can hardly be attributed to divestiture.

The jump from correlation to causation is obviously very risky at the policy prescription level if undue credit is given to the act of divestiture. For example, a relevant policy prescription in the case of Aeromexico could have been posed in terms of ways to relax the regulatory restrictions that made bankruptcy the only option for the survival of the firm, rather than simply crediting favorable results to divestiture. A similar comment applies to Telmex, in which the relaxation of labor contract constraints took the form of a concession to the union of a 4.4 percent slice of the company. Obviously this concession does not have to be related to divestiture, as the government can follow—and has followed in other nondivestiture cases—similar procedures to make labor contracts more flexible, thereby enhancing productivity.

What will happen? The limitations of the package type approach to the analysis of divestiture carry over to the treatment of the factual (divestiture) and counterfactual (nondivestiture) projections. The methodology here is an interesting one, but there are problems and risks. Many of the structural changes that have taken place in Mexico (such as price deregulation in the telephone sector) would likely have occurred even without divestiture. It would have been instructive to elaborate on these exercises, perhaps at the expense of some descriptive sections. One way to do this would be to construct more than one factual projection (as was done only in the case of Aeromexico), to isolate the distinctive roles of essential factors and make the counterfactual scenarios more realistic.

Also in the Aeromexico case, the researchers note the doubling of labor productivity after divestiture, ostensibly associated with sharp reductions in employment, and claim that the rise would have been impossible without divestiture. They conclude, therefore, "that the dramatic increase in labor productivity is definitely due to divestiture." While the statement is true in terms of correlations, it overlooks the real factor that allowed the reduction of employment: the elimination through bankruptcy of labor contract rigidities that followed from rigidities in the labor laws.

What was it worth? Alternative scenarios and simulations of the kind described above would have provided better guidance for interpreting the numerical results on welfare changes. Such sensitivity analysis is important because the studies now leave the impression that the results necessarily follow "by construction." But some assumptions in the factual projections may be irrelevant and some may belong in the counterfactual. The reader, however, cannot tell.

The final sections on the Mexico cases are perhaps the most disappointing. The conclusions are hardly surprising and seem to require only qualitative assessments of the implications of the policy measures that accompany divestiture. So what was the purpose of all of those quantitative estimates, one wonders. While economists usually feel more secure with quantitative estimates, the level of generality in the case studies when they come to the policy prescription level throws into question the merits of such a long numerical journey. My suggestion is not to ignore the quantitative results, but to exploit more fully the effort to derive conclusions that are derivable only from welfare calculations.

While my comments have dealt with some of the shortcomings of the study, I want to make clear that I believe that this study has made a remarkable contribution to our knowledge of divestiture, particularly the application of a rigorous methodology for measuring the welfare effects of privatization. The study will certainly play a major role in expanding our understanding of one of today's key policy issues.

Eliana Cardoso

Not all developing countries have demonstrated an equal commitment to free markets. Most of them use the right rhetoric about privatization, but few have actually reformed their public sector. Among the most successful reformers are Chile, which disposed of 470 public enterprises, and Mexico, which disposed of 700.

I share Tandon's view that privatization was instrumental in restoring growth in Mexico. Revenues from the sales were used to reduce government debt, restore confidence, and improve the investment climate.

In general, several arguments can be made for privatization. One argument that is not made often enough but that was recognized by

Mexican policymakers is that privatization relaxes the credit constraint faced by governments. Where the public sector faces severe credit rationing, maintenance and capacity expansion do not take place, leading to a weakening of infrastructure that reduces the profitability and competitiveness of private investment as well. Thus the private sector and foreign investors, which do not face credit rationing, are better suited to conducting operations that require major investments, such as airlines, telecommunications, ports, and highways. Privatization released an investment constraint in all three cases in Mexico. Welfare improved in the cases of Telmex and Aeromexico, but declined in the case of Mexicana.

Another argument for privatization rests on the belief that private production is more efficient because it offers a better incentive structure than does public ownership. Efficiency requires that managers have a direct personal stake in the profitability of their enterprises, something that is lacking in public enterprises, where commercial objectives are subordinated to political goals and the threat of bankruptcy is absent. In contrast, efficient capital markets capitalize the consequences of current actions under a private ownership regime. But the evidence on capital market efficiency is mixed, and governments can loosen a firm's budget constraints by offering subsidies, trade protection, and loan guarantees. In the case of monopolies, the welfare effects of privatization depend on successful regulation. But regulation may reintroduce the problem that privatization was supposed to cure: public officials acting in their own interest.

What do the three case studies show? For Aeromexico, the key change following divestiture was that the company broke even for two years instead of being the heavy money-loser and fiscal drain it had been before divestiture. Labor productivity increased and consumers lost. The big winner was the government, which shed a money-losing firm.

Proving the point that pigs cannot fly even when they are privately operated is Mexicana Airlines. The government avoided losses, but both foreigners and consumers are worse off because of an overambitious investment program.

In the case of Telmex, profits and total factor productivity have been increasing since 1988, with a notable 15 percent increase in productivity in 1991, the first year after divestiture. Domestic and foreign shareholders gained, but consumers were big losers. The fiscal impact was positive, and government enjoyed the benefits of the rising stock market valuation of the firm in the form of higher per share sale revenues on successive offers. That rising stock market value is the most dramatic change brought about by the privatization. The stock rose twenty-five-fold in four years. Tandon's estimate of the private value of Telmex is roughly double the stock market value. Calling that estimate conservative, he concludes that the market is not anticipating any huge efficiency improvements and, rather, perceives some risk in the stock. I find that conclusion surprising.

The valuation of the telephone company involves four issues. First, the case study argues that Telmex stock has risen much faster than the market overall, which suggests that the telephone company must be seen as a growth stock. The second issue is the value of the franchise, the exclusive right to supply telephone services ranging from installation to domestic and international calls. The value is affected by several factors, including expanding technological possibilities for undermining Telmex's monopoly (U.S. direct-style services, competition from alternative carriers entering under the guise of deregulation, and new satellite technology offering the possibility of using world carriers, to name some).

The third consideration is the cost of doing business, specifically the prospects for dramatic increases in productivity. It is doubtful, though, that the three come together in the case of Mexico. It is unlikely that we can look forward to a decade of costless gains in productivity of the kind that took place in 1991. Without the same 15 percent a year increase in productivity and with a porous franchise, even strong growth of the Mexican economy is not enough to warrant a $55 billion dollar Telmex. Reflect a moment. If Telmex is worth $55 billion, Telebras of Brazil is worth $96 billion, and that means that country has no debt problem—it just gives its creditors the telephone franchise.

Fourth, is a miracle good or bad news for Telmex? The combination of deregulation and innovation is the biggest threat to big profits and monopolies. Witness the experience of the United States, where bank franchises have become worthless and where cutthroat competition in telecommunications has benefited consumers, not stockholders. Mexico may well witness much the same outcome in banking, telecommunications, and air transport.

Economists focus on the benefits to consumers from innovation, entry, and competition. In capital markets, the first question should be who is going to lose his shirt? The combined value of the telephone companies of Greece, Italy, Portugal, and Spain is less than the value of Telmex today. Considering that these countries together are bigger than Mexico in both population and income, it seems that Telmex stock reflects not only its anticipated profit flows, but also the fact that more people want a piece of the Mexican pie today.

So what is the most important lesson of privatization in Mexico? The success of privatization programs in Mexico—and in Chile— demonstrates that privatization is merely one act in a larger play, a lesson most developing countries have been slow to grasp. The reversal of decades of statism in Chile has created the basis of arguably the healthiest economy in Latin America. Nonetheless, policy errors that required the government to bail out financial institutions in the recession of 1982 underline the need for a more consistent approach to privatization. Mexico's privatization scheme stands as a more rational and well-conceptualized method of reducing the size of the state.

8

MALAYSIA

Leroy Jones

Welcome to the real world. So far, we have talked about superstars: the United Kingdom, the pacesetter, and Chile and Mexico, the big privatizers of the developing world, which account for some 900 of the 1,300 or so divestitures in developing countries (excluding Eastern Europe). That leaves about 500 divestitures for the other 100 or so developing countries, or about 5 per country. Malaysia has divested tens of enterprises rather than hundreds, which puts it above the average for this group, but well below Chile and Mexico.

Malaysia's divestitures share one important characteristic with those in other developing countries: many of its divestitures—and two of the three case studies—were partial. The government did not sell 100 percent of the equity or relinquish control to the private purchaser, except in the case of the lottery. The two partial divestitures, Malaysian Airline Systems and Kelang Container Terminal, show that success is possible even through a partial, step-by-step process. What Malaysia has done in these cases, it has done well.

Malaysia's experience also resembles that of Chile and Mexico in certain ways. All three countries have a roughly equivalent income per capita, have had reasonably high growth rates since the divestitures started, and have governments that are actively engaged in other reforms as well as divestiture.

An important goal of economic policy in Malaysia that needs to be considered in any analysis of reform measures is redistribution of economic power to the Bumiputeras, the ethnic Malays. It is not just welfare in the aggregate but also the distribution of the welfare that matters from an economic policy perspective.

Malaysian Airline Systems

Malaysian Airline Systems is a sibling of Singapore Airlines, one of the best airlines in the world. Malaysian Air separated from its parent only about eighteen years ago. True to its genetic stock, Malaysian Air was a well-run airline before its divestiture, which, as in the case of the two Chilean electricity companies, reduced the scope for improvement after divestiture. The airline has a monopoly domestically, but faces some competition internationally. As is often the case with national lines, Malaysian Air has a tendency to use profits on international routes to subsidize its domestic services.

In this partial divestiture, the government retained 42 percent of the shares, other public enterprises had 10 percent, state governments had 10 percent, and employees had 5 percent. Fifteen percent of the shares were sold on the stock market, and after the initial issue an additional 18 percent were sold to foreigners, most to the government of Brunei.

What happened? Inside the firm, virtually nothing changed with divestiture. Management continued to do more or less the same things it had been doing. What did change were the investment constraints binding the firm, the same story as in the British Telecom, Chile Telecom, and Telmex cases.

We expect the divestiture to affect the government's response when it reviews price decisions of Malaysian Air now that there are a substantial number of private shareholders. This is, of course, conjecture only. The government allowed no increase in domestic prices from 1982 through 1991. As the profitability of the firm drops, it will eventually reach such a low point that the government will have to approve a price increase. That would be true whether ownership were private or public. What we expect to be different, though, is that the trip wire will go off sooner after divestiture. In 1982 profitability fell to minus 23 percent before the government allowed a reasonable domestic price increase. We think that private shareholders, including the government of Brunei, will not let profitability sink that low before they demand a domestic price increase. So we project that under a privatized Malaysian Air, domestic air fares will be higher than they would be had the airline remained fully publicly owned.

Who won and who lost? Domestic consumers lost 3 percent; foreign consumers gained a little (figure 8.1). Domestic consumers lost because they faced higher prices. But higher prices do not necessarily indicate exploitation of consumers. In the Malaysian Airline Systems case, the higher prices reflect only a partial reduction of inefficient pricing subsidies. Domestic prices remain well below international levels, but the price increases are at least a step in the direction of more efficient pricing. So although consumers lose because of the higher prices, they also gain from the expanded investment, which led to reduced waiting times and easier access to planes.

Foreigners gained slightly as well because of the loosening of the investment constraint, which worked in the following way. About the only way to get to Malaysia is on Singapore Airlines or Malaysian Air. The two airlines have an agreement to share this route 50-50, a form

Figure 8.1 Kelang Container Terminal: Who Won: Who Lost?

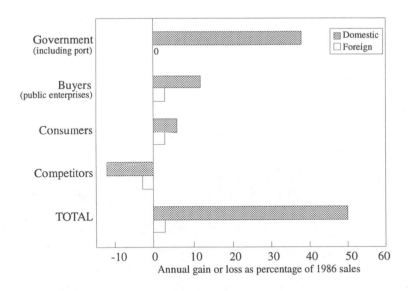

Annual gain or loss as percentage of 1986 sales

Source: Jones, Leroy, and Fadil Azim Abbas, with contributions from Yong-Min Chen, "Malaysia," in Ahmeds Galal, Leroy Jones, Pankaj Tandon, and Ingo Vogelsang, *Welfare Consequences of Selling Public Enterprises: Case Studies from Chile, Malaysia, Mexico and the United Kingdom* (New York: Oxford University Press, forthcoming).

of market sharing common among international airlines. There are two possible outcomes for Singapore Air when Malaysian Air is unable to invest. One is that Singapore Air benefits by filling the gap. The other—and this is the outcome we project—is that the Malaysian government does not grant the extra landing rights to Singapore Airlines until Malaysian Air can meet 50 percent of the demand itself. So when there is an investment constraint on Malaysian Air, Singapore Airlines suffers too. And when the constraint is lifted foreign competitors like Singapore Airline gain along with Malaysian Air.

Thus gains from divestiture are possible even when an enterprise is reasonably well run to begin with because external changes are also critical. If the government exercises its regulatory power more intelligently after divestiture as a result of the pressures imposed by private shareholders, that is a step in the right direction. If it exercises its powers to approve investments in a more economically rational fashion, then there are welfare gains.

Kelang Container Terminal

The privatization of Kelang Container Terminal involved a breakup of a larger enterprise. The government put a fence down the middle of the terminal, with eight wharves on one side, and one wharf, the container terminal, on the other. Some workers were on one side of the fence, some were on the other. At first, the workers opposed the divestiture. Afterward, however, workers and union leaders on both sides of the fence were singing the praises of divestiture. Now their only complaint is that the whole port wasn't privatized.

Another interesting point about the breakup is, as one union leader put it, "They sold the gold mine and kept the coal mine." The divested container terminal accounted for more than half the profit, but only a little more than 10 percent of the work force and other costs. Forty-nine percent of the shares were held by the old port; 41 percent by another public enterprise, a general transport company; and 10 percent went to a private foreign firm, PNO, an Australian shipping company with considerable experience in ports and shipping transport. The company provided a key input—technological know-how—for a very low price.

Kelang Container Terminal faces some competition. One competitor is container shipping through Singapore, although coverage is limited. The major competition is from conventional shipping through the parent company, which also owns 49 percent of the container terminal.

In general, things turned around very well after privatization. Before divestiture Kelang had one particularly good year, but otherwise did not do very well. After divestiture, profits rose from about 2 percent a year to 12 percent. Productivity growth jumped from about 5 percent to 18 percent annually.

What accounted for the change? Primarily, the new private management. The new managers provided strong incentives. Real wages rose some 70 percent, and labor has been involved in management decisions. People are working harder, producing two to two and a half times as much as before. Turnaround time has dropped substantially, boosting the rate of containerization. The cost of intermediate inputs has fallen dramatically too as workers use their idle time to perform intermediate services once provided by outsiders. It is hard to say how much of the turnaround was due to the technical advice provided by PNO Australia, but clearly much of it was—from better production scheduling to better yard organization.

So Kelang shows how divestiture can make a public enterprise internally more efficient—the reverse of the case of Malaysian Air. Kelang also differs from the Malaysian Air case in the absence of price effects (price increases weren't needed) and investment effects (investments had already been planned under the public sector). Kelang also demonstrates that even partial divestiture can have big payoffs. All the changes occurred while the government still owned 90 percent of the shares. For a relatively small percentage of foreign equity, Kelang got an enormous response.

In terms of the bottom line, the government and the buyers did well, but the government was the big winner (figure 8.2). Consumers came out a little ahead, and competitors lost a little bit.

The lessons here are that partial divestiture can be more than cosmetic. The government managed a controlled exercise in market power. An interesting point is that the turnaround was so dramatic, perhaps because it's easier to see dramatic change in a small firm—

Figure 8.2 Malaysian Airline Systems: Who Won? Who Lost?

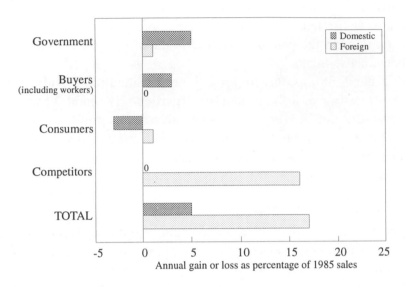

Source: Jones, Leroy, and Fadil Azim Abbas, with contributions from Yong-Min Chen, "Malaysia," in Ahmeds Galal, Leroy Jones, Pankaj Tandon, and Ingo Vogelsang, *Welfare Consequences of Selling Public Enterprises: Case Studies from Chile, Malaysia, Mexico and the United Kingdom* (New York: Oxford University Press, forthcoming).

Kelang has 800 workers—than in a big one. These were the same workers as before, but better management and better incentives motivated them to work harder.

Lottery—Sports Toto

The third case is a lottery, quite a different entity than the others in this study. Sports Toto is a revenue monopoly, which means that the government is not concerned with preventing exploitation of consumers. Indeed, exploitation of consumers is the point. Why would the government sell a revenue monopoly? I am advised by people who know Malaysia that the government sold the lottery because of rising religious opposition to gambling. So, unlike the other cases in Malaysia, the lottery sale was a complete divestiture.

What happened as a result? Would the government raise more money by running the lottery or by selling it to the private sector and taxing the returns? The issue here is who is better at exploiting the consumer. It turns out that the private sector is much better at exploiting consumers than is the government because it is much better at marketing and advertising products. The new owners developed new products, did a lot of marketing and franchising, established fancy new stalls—all the dynamic and innovative things expected of private sector owners. Over the next four years, sales tripled, public profits quadrupled, and government revenue tripled, all in real terms (figure 8.3).

The bulk of the gains came at the expense of other companies, considerably reducing the net welfare effect (figure 8.4). Sports Toto's share of the revenues from gambling rose substantially, but its competitors did worse, and the government lost a bit from its take on that side.

Little can be said about what happened to consumers, for several reasons. For one, we had no data on the lottery's payout rate since the company would not let us look at their books. And even if we had the data, economic analysis does not really provide us with a way of assessing welfare from gambling—if you gamble more, are you better or worse off?—or of judging changes induced by advertising—if advertising convinces consumers to buy this product rather than another one, are they better off? So we viewed this divestiture as primarily a case of government revenue generation.

This case suggests that divestiture might yield particularly high gains in activities that require advertising, marketing, innovation, quick decisions, and responsiveness, modes of action to which the government is ill-suited. Among the activities with these characteristics are export marketing, foreign sales, tourism and running hotels, and revenue monopolies.

Conclusion

What contribution did the divestitures make to the government's goal of improving the welfare of the Bumiputeras? Did divestiture increase the share of the economy controlled by ethnic Malays? Simply selling shares exclusively to the Bumiputeras would not improve their position since the money they spent on one company is money they could no longer spend on another. And at normal market

Figure 8.3 Sports Toto: Details of Real Fiscal Effects

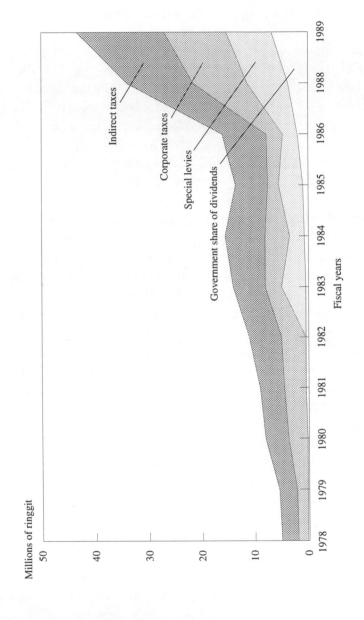

Millions of ringgit

Indirect taxes

Corporate taxes

Special levies

Government share of dividends

Fiscal years

Source: Jones, Leroy, and Fadil Azim Abbas, with contributions from Yong-Min Chen, "Malaysia," in Ahmeds Galal, Leroy Jones, Pankaj Tandon, and Ingo Vogelsang, *Welfare Consequences of Selling Public Enterprises: Case Studies from Chile, Malaysia, Mexico and the United Kingdom* (New York: Oxford University Press, forthcoming).

Figure 8.4 Sports Toto: Who Won? Who Lost?

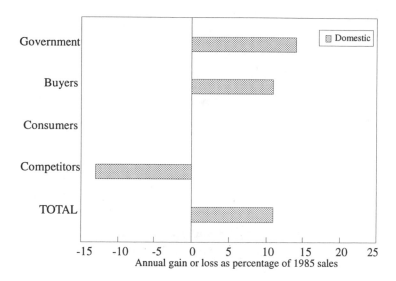

Source: Jones, Leroy, and Fadil Azim Abbas, with contributions from Yong-Min Chen, "Malaysia," in Ahmeds Galal, Leroy Jones, Pankaj Tandon, and Ingo Vogelsang, *Welfare Consequences of Selling Public Enterprises: Case Studies from Chile, Malaysia, Mexico and the United Kingdom* (New York: Oxford University Press, forthcoming).

rates, the return would be the same as on shares of some other company. So if it is a market-based transaction, there is no gain to the Bumiputeras. But there is a way to tilt the outcome in their favor, and that is to sell shares at below-market value to the Bumiputeras—and only to them. Selling shares at subsidized prices may induce people who would not otherwise have done so to buy shares, thereby expanding people's capitalism and achieving real gains for the Bumiputeras. So there are gains in this system for the Malays who receive special access to underpriced shares, both the rich and the middle class, but the gains are somewhat less than is generally supposed.

A key lesson of the Malaysia cases concerns the gains from partial divestiture. Whatever the reason for partial rather than full divestiture—political constraints, income distribution, economic circumstances—the gains can be substantial if the divestiture is intelligently planned.

Comments

Ijaz Nabi

These three case studies provide rich detail on the criteria for looking at and measuring the gains from privatization. The next time I use the word *privatization*, it will be backed up by the confidence I have gained from these three case studies. But, I hasten to add, the case studies answer only some of the questions about privatization. The larger issue is the effect on overall economic efficiency and competitiveness.

In the early 1980s Malaysia was not the model of macroeconomic stability it is viewed as today. Malaysia had run up a huge fiscal deficit of nearly 19 percent of GNP, inflation was high by East Asian standards, the ratio of debt to GNP was almost 145 percent in 1983-84, and economic growth had slowed. The government's presence in the economy was enormous, with government expenditures accounting for nearly 49 percent of GNP. And nearly half the state enterprises were running losses.

This was the context that prompted the decision to privatize some state enterprises. The architects of the new economic plan—you can't talk about Malaysia in the last twenty years without talking about the new economic plan—were keenly aware that the plan's objectives would not be met without a resumption of growth. Privatization posed a special problem because public enterprises also serve a redistributional function in Malaysia by providing employment for the Bumiputeras. Policymakers realized that sooner or later the only way to fulfill the underlying objectives of the new economic plan would be to see that the Bumiputeras received assets that would engage them in the economy as entrepreneurs. In turn, that would require opening up the economy, increasing investment opportunities, and making the entire economic structure more competitive.

This context focuses attention on certain impacts of the privatization process that began in Malaysia in 1984-85. Did privatization reduce the government's presence in the economy? Was there less regulation and more competition? Had financial and administrative burdens lightened? Did enterprise performance improve? And was there greater asset ownership by the Bumiputeras?

In the case of Malaysia Airline Systems, the government sold shares but retained control. Government revenue went up; company performance improved, primarily as a result of output and investment expansion, but also because of the price increases on domestic routes; and shareholders gained. Domestic consumers lost, but foreign consumers, shareholders, and competitors gained.

These results and the way they are interpreted raise some issues in my mind. If foreign consumers benefited from an expansion in routes, should that be considered a leakage to foreign competition? Had the shares in Malaysia Airline Systems not been sold, would the government have allowed the airline to increase its investment? In light of the fiscal picture in Malaysia, I am convinced that that would not have happened. The government had made a fundamental decision to cut back on expenditures, so I think that the counterfactual simulation with increased government investment in the airline can simply be ruled out.

In the Kelang Container Terminal case, most of the benefits came from gains in productivity, the result of higher wages and better management practices that improved worker-management relations. This is an interesting effect, and it has an important bearing on the future of privatization in Malaysia. Malaysia's labor market is becoming increasingly tight, and the country will need to focus on productivity growth in order to sustain economic growth.

Donald Snodgrass

Malaysia's new economic policy defined very explicit redistributive goals. The redistribution was to take place at the margin, and economic growth was to be maintained. The outcome has been remarkable. Over the twenty years of the plan, Malaysia was able to maintain one of the highest average growth rates among developing countries while achieving a substantial proportion of its redistribution and poverty-alleviation targets.

The privatization policy came to the fore in 1983, early in the second decade of this policy framework, and was, as Ijaz Nabi indicated, a reaction to the setbacks of the early 1980s. Privatization was intended to improve the fiscal position of the government and increase the efficiency and productivity of the enterprises so they could contribute more to growth. The Kelang Container Terminal was carefully chosen as the first to be divested because the container port was operating inefficiently, with assumed high social costs to the economy. The question of the new economic plan and the distribution of ownership shares to the Bumiputeras also came into the picture. In fact, public enterprises had been established in the first place primarily as a way of increasing the Bumiputeras' participation in the economy. More than 400 public enterprises were created in the 1970s and another 200 or so in the early 1980s.

The question, then, was how to divest in a way that would strike an acceptable balance among these differing and not necessarily consistent goals. As Leroy Jones pointed out, using divestiture to increase the Bumiputeras' share in capital holdings requires underpricing the shares in some way, which, of course, runs up against the government's revenue-raising objective.

Certain characteristics of the Malaysian experience with privatization stand out. It has moved rather slowly relative to what the government has said it wants to do. The divestitures have usually been partial; the government has not generally been willing to give up control. Most of the privatized enterprises have been natural monopolies. And in some cases, assets appear to have been transferred to private interests at less than market value.

Productivity rose in two of the three cases studied here. The explanations for the rise seem somewhat ad hoc. In the case of Kelang Container Terminal the government seems to have been fortunate in the quality of the new Australian management. The simple street version of what happened is that the Australian bosses were able to make people work harder than the Malaysian bosses had been able to do. In the case of Sports Toto, the word on the street is that the turnaround was simply a matter of replacing lethargic civil servants with capable and aggressive business people.

The case of Malaysian Airline Systems is different. Conventional wisdom is that the divestiture could not have increased productivity since only part of the stock was sold; there was no change in management. It is interesting, then, and certainly a sign of a research payoff, that the researchers are able to establish, at least to my satisfaction, that even though management did not change, divestiture had an important effect on operations through a greater willingness to finance expansion.

The performance of Kelang Container Terminal improved markedly after divestiture. I think the anecdotal evidence of a substantial improvement in management supports the conclusion of the study that the gains are attributable mainly to divestiture. Though the foreign ownership share of the company was small, the change in management appears to have been critical. The study notes that after divestiture, growth of traffic volume at the terminal outpaced growth of GDP, which seems to reflect the increasing competitiveness of the container port relative to conventional cargo handling at Kelang or the cost of going through Singapore.

I see two principal lessons in the Malaysian cases. One is that the government may have very different motives for undertaking divestiture than those of the World Bank and other international agencies. Those particular motives are likely to affect the results of divestiture. Another lesson is that efficiency may rise even if improved efficiency is not the original aim. One thing the Malaysian cases suggest is that combining politically correct ownership with competent professional management can produce results in politically complex circumstances.

PART 3

SYNTHESIS
AND
POLICY IMPLICATIONS

9

WINNERS AND LOSERS IN PRIVATIZATION

Leroy Jones

Two patterns emerge from the case studies: patterns of distribution, or what happened to various groups, and patterns of explanations, or why particular sets of distributional results came about. Before addressing these two issues, note that we find positive welfare changes in eleven of twelve cases. Thus, I'd like to start by looking at the outliers, particularly the lone loser, Mexicana Airlines. Is this a case of a failure of divestiture? I don't think so. In fact, I think it demonstrates one of the strengths of divestiture.

Recall what happened. The new private capitalists, giving free rein to their animal spirits, went out and overinvested in a declining market. They also put too much heavy paint on their planes and made several other bad decisions. Basically, they just didn't display good business sense.

The private sector has automatic mechanisms for turning around loss-making business, all the way to the end of the line, which is bankruptcy. In the public sector, losses go on for years. Mexicana and Aeromexico had been draining money from the federal budget for a long time.

The outlier on the gainer side is Chile Telecom. The interesting thing here is that Chile Telecom is another story about investment. When Mexicana's new owners increased investment, it was the wrong thing to do. When Chile Telecom's owners did so, it was the right thing to do. Output doubled in about four years, with substantial gains for consumers.

Chile Telecom, like British Telecom and Malaysia Airline System, is a case in which the release of the investment constraint was a major source of the gains from privatization. In some large enterprises, new investments reduced the high costs to consumers of such inefficiencies as two-year waits for telephone installation and electricity brownouts and blackouts.

Consumers

One of the arguments for public enterprises is the fear that the private sector will exploit consumers where there is monopoly or oligopoly power. From that fear follows the concern that divestiture may lead not only to more efficient operation, but also to more efficient exploitation of consumers.

Indeed, consumers did lose in some cases (figure 9.1). The dramatic losses were all in Mexico, although there were small losses to consumers in the United Kingdom and Malaysia. I will focus on Mexico, however, because that is where the big numbers are.

Is the loss to consumers—primarily because of higher prices—an indication of a failure of divestiture? No, because the loss derives not from exploitation of market power but from price increases reflecting a shift from high subsidies to economically rational pricing. So although the rise in prices from uneconomically low levels hurt consumers in the first round, in most cases this loss was offset quickly by increased investment and expansion that reduced waiting time and rationing.

But, it can be further argued, doesn't the move toward rational pricing worsen income distribution? I submit that that has not happened in most cases. It's not the poor who were flying on the airlines or consuming telephone or electricity services in Mexico, but the upper and middle classes. Raising the prices of services such as these generates revenue that can be used to expand these services or to provide better public education or health benefits.

If we consider the welfare effects of only the price change—our projections assume several changes at once, from differences in prices to differences in investment and employment—we find that the effect is almost universally positive. British Airways is the only case in which the price changes associated with divestiture significantly hurt the

Figure 9.1 Welfare Gains and Losses to Domestic Consumers

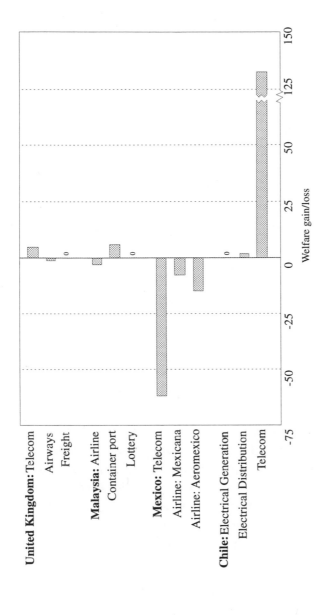

Notes: All figures are the annual component of perpetuity equivalent to the welfare change (ACPE), expressed as a percentage of annual sales in the last pre-divestiture year. The figure for workers includes both their role as wage earners and as buyers of shares.

Source: Galal, Ahmed, Leroy Jones, Pankaj Tandon, and Ingo Vogelsang, *Welfare Consequences of Selling Public Enterprises: Case Studies from Chile, Malaysia, Mexico and the United Kingdom* (New York: Oxford University Press, forthcoming).

economy. The merger of British Airways and Caledonia, which we attribute in part to divestiture, allowed the exploitation of market power in the domestic market, with a consequent loss in welfare as prices rose. But everywhere else, particularly in Mexico, the losses to consumers were more than offset by gains to other groups as a consequence of moving toward a more efficient set of prices.

Workers

Another group often said to lose from divestiture is workers (figure 9.2). Is their fear of divestiture justified? We found not a single case in which divestiture made workers worse off. In a number of cases, workers did better, whether through higher wages or through share purchases in the privatized company. Even after making adjustments for workers who lost their jobs (taking into account their severance pay, expected time out of work, and expected earnings when they go back to work), we found no case in which employees overall are worse off as a result of divestiture. Workers generally have some power to negotiate a favorable deal during privatization. Most public enterprises are reasonably high-tech operations, requiring employees with technical skills. That gives workers who were there before privatization some leverage during the negotiations, which has allowed them to do reasonably well.

Profits

What pattern do we find for profits, defined as all returns to capital whether reserved by the equity holder, the debt holder, or the government? Again, all results are positive (figure 9.3). Profits went up, efficiency went up. And they went up a lot more in Malaysia and Mexico than in Chile and the United Kingdom. The reason for that difference was most clearly identified in the Chilean case studies, but it applies as well to those in the United Kingdom. These enterprises were simply better run to begin with. In poorer countries there is a lot more room for improvement because the gap in performance between public and private enterprises is larger.

The gains in profits came in large part from increased productivity, and much of the productivity gain came from shedding excess labor. The most dramatic case was Aeromexico. But there were major

Figure 9.2 Welfare Gains and Losses to Domestic Workers

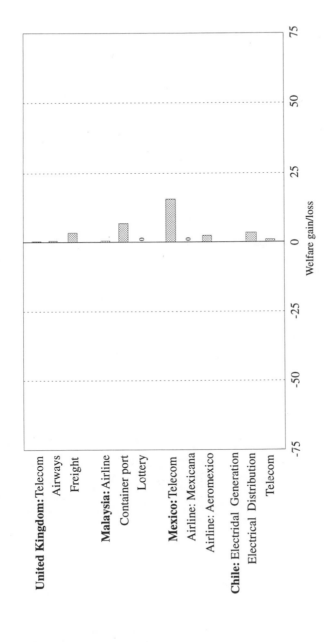

Notes: All figures are the annual component of perpetuity equivalent to the welfare change (ACPE), expressed as a percentage of annual sales in the last pre-divestiture year. The figure for workers includes both their role as wage earners and as buyers of shares.

Source: Galal, Ahmed, Leroy Jones, Pankaj Tandon, and Ingo Vogelsang, *Welfare Consequences of Selling Public Enterprises: Case Studies from Chile, Malaysia, Mexico and the United Kingdom* (New York: Oxford University Press, forthcoming).

Figure 9.3 Gains and Losses

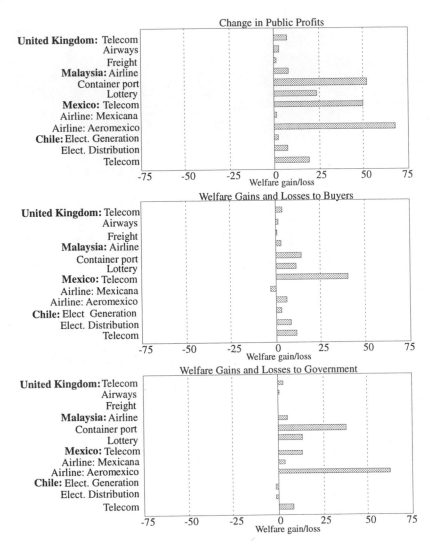

Notes: All figures are the annual component of perpetuity equivalent to the welfare change (ACPE), expressed as a percentage of annual sales in the last pre-divestiture year. The figure for workers includes both their role as wage earners and as buyers of shares.

Source: Galal, Ahmed, Leroy Jones, Pankaj Tandon, and Ingo Vogelsang, *Welfare Consequences of Selling Public Enterprises: Case Studies from Chile, Malaysia, Mexico and the United Kingdom* (New York: Oxford University Press, forthcoming).

productivity gains from more broadly defined management reforms as well. The Kelang Container Terminal divestiture presents the strongest case for the efficacy of management reforms.

Product quality or diversification improved substantially in several cases as well. The Malaysian lottery, Sports Toto, shows what large changes can flow from improving and expanding services. It suggests that enterprises that deal with the public and in which marketing and personal service are important are especially likely to show large gains from privatization.

Profits rose everywhere. Their distribution between buyer and seller depends on the selling price and any additional terms and conditions, such as taxes and special levies (figure 9.3). Buyers did pretty well except in the case of Mexicana Airlines, where the buyers paid a price for their poor management decisions. With the exception of Telmex, where the buyers reaped large gains, variance in buyer profits across the case studies is surprisingly low. It may be that buyers believe that market forces work, so they are willing to pay no more than the price that allows them a return above their opportunity costs. They are entering into a risky venture, so they require a return above their opportunity cost. Governments have done a fairly good job of keeping buyers from getting really large excess returns by regulating the terms down to a level just above the buyers' opportunity costs.

On the seller's side, variance is considerably greater. Governments have gotten especially high returns in Malaysia and Mexico (figure 9.3). Part of the reason is that the gains from divestiture were greater than in Chile and the United Kingdom, so there were more profits to distribute. In Mexico the government ceded considerable control, but few of the benefits, early on. The government kept some shares in trust or as sequestered, nonvoting shares, allowing the private sector to make management decisions and the government to retain the benefits by selling those shares downstream, when their value had increased. Malaysia relied on a variety of profit-sharing mechanisms, especially taxes and special levies. Both governments did a good job of negotiating a large share of profits for themselves. The important question in terms of income distribution is what governments do with these profits. If the funds are used to help the poor by investing in education and health services, divestiture will have a positive effect on income distribution and the poor.

In the two Chilean cases in which government returns were negative, did that indicate that divestiture was a mistake? Well, perhaps the Chilean government could have bargained harder. But, really, the gains to be had there were small. Moreover, would an intelligent government be willing to spend $100 million to get $500 million for society? Governments do this all the time. They invest in roads, education, health services, putting out the money for others' gain. The same thing happened here. Society as a whole benefited, and the government paid a price.

Other groups were also affected. These include both the competitors who lost in the Kelang Terminal and lottery sales, and the existing shareholders in Telmex and Mexicana, who, though not included among the new buyers, gained as the shares rose in value after divestiture.

On balance, the bulk of the gains from divestiture went to domestic groups. In the case of Kelang Container Terminal, some of the benefits went to PNO Australia. To a considerable extent it was PNO's technical knowledge that generated the benefits, so the price was a small one. The exception is Telmex. The bulk of the benefits went to foreigners, an outcome that is more a political than an economic concern.

Conclusion

These patterns of effects show that divestiture has clearly been a successful policy if not a perfect one. The only perfect policies are in textbooks. If all the policy changes made by government were as successful as these divestitures, the world would be a far better place.

Relatively few other generalizations can be made about the divestitures, and the reason is fairly simple. Divestiture is a move toward control by market forces, a push toward more efficient mechanisms. But the direction of that push depends on the starting point and the distortions in the economy. These distortions have been quite different, and so the pressures imposed by markets have been quite different. Although the net impact of market forces has been positive, the nature of the impact depends on the circumstances.

For that reason, I don't think we can use the results of the study to predict results elsewhere. Even in countries similar to those in the sample, the results will not be exactly the same. Nor would we necessarily predict the same kinds of results in poorer countries or in Eastern European countries, where markets are just emerging, as in our sample of middle-income countries, with their relatively good governments and relatively well-developed markets and human resources.

Although we cannot use the results of the study for prediction, I think we can use them for prescription, to talk about what successful divestiture requires. Successful divestiture is not a single policy decision, but an integrated package of a large number of individual decisions. These case studies show, by and large, what things have to be done right to make divestiture work.

10

POLICY IMPLICATIONS

Ahmed Galal

The case studies clearly show that gains from divestiture can be substantial. Implicit in that finding is that ownership matters. But so does policy. Getting the deal done does not make the difference. Getting it done right and in the right environment does. For example, was the trade regime liberalized before a public enterprise producing tradable commodities was sold? Were regulations in place before a monopoly was privatized? How was the deal structured? These are important dimensions of divestiture policy that make a difference for the outcomes.

There are no blueprints that guarantee that divestiture will come out right. There are some common ground rules, however, that have been derived from research and practical experience and that apply just about everywhere. These guidelines offer some answers to four of the common concerns about divestiture policy:

- Which enterprises should be sold and in what order? (Small firms first? Profitable or less profitable firms? What about monopolies?)
- How should they be sold, and should they be restructured first?
- Does it matter to whom the enterprises are sold?
- When should the process start?

Which Enterprises to Sell

We know from simple observations of divestitures around the world that most countries started with smaller firms. In fact, Mexico and Chile sold hundreds of small enterprises in a relatively short time early in their divestiture programs. What makes this strategy logical?

Small firms don't have market power, so they cannot exploit consumers. The number of bidders is potentially large because the value of these firms is relatively small. It is also easier to turn around a small company. The Kelang Container Terminal in Malaysia is a good example of that. Another advantage is that a large number of firms can be sold at the beginning of the process of privatization, enabling the government to shed many of its enterprises at once. Cutting down sharply on the number of public enterprises releases scarce government resources to focus on the things that only governments can do.

The only hitch is that the gains from privatizing small enterprises are likely to be small as well. For that reason, a government might want to start with larger firms instead. Privatizing a telecommunications company is likely to have a big impact on the rest of the economy. So there is a case for starting big. But big sometimes means monopoly power. In that case, the gains can still be substantial, but a regulatory framework needs to be in place before the firm is sold. Moreover, the capital market may not be able to absorb such a large sale, which can be dealt with by allowing foreign participation.

Irrespective of which enterprise is finally chosen for sale first, competition and regulation are critical for success. In the case of enterprises in tradable sectors, like steel and fertilizer, policymakers can make a difference by introducing competition before selling the firm—by liberalizing trade or liberalizing entry into the markets in which the firm operates. Failure to permit competition will allow the producer to make money no matter how the firm is run.

In the case of nontradables, for example, electricity and telecommunications services, there are also possibilities for introducing competition. For instance, while there are economies of scale in the provision of local telephone services, the same is not true for the sale of phone equipment or for value-added services. Therefore, it would pay off to allow competition in the latter markets. Similarly, while electricity distribution involves economies of scale, electricity generation does not. Therefore, separating electricity generation from distribution before divestiture, as Chile did, is commendable from the point of view of enhancing competition.

Even with such efforts, however, there will always be some monopolies that will have to be regulated. In this regard, two elements are particularly important: pricing and regulatory institutions. As for pricing, Mexico and the United Kingdom applied the RPI minus x price cap formula. The model used by Chile relies on a rate of return, but one that is based on an efficient firm. There are other models too. The point is that this is an area where an investment in searching out good solutions would be justified. Establishing independent regulatory bodies, as did Chile and the United Kingdom, is also worth considering. These should not be just another government department. They need to be set up as independent bodies, free of political interference.

How to Sell

Aside from restructuring markets to enhance competition, should a firm be restructured before it is sold? There is an apparent illogic in restructuring an enterprise before selling it. Privatization implies a belief that the private sector can do a better job of turning the company around than can the public sector. So why not leave the task to those who will do the better job?

Restructuring that involves large investments, such as installing a new plant, would be a case in point. And, indeed, none of the firms studied was restructured in that way before its sale. But there are other types of restructuring that do make sense before divestiture.

Sometimes legal restructuring is required before divestiture. In all the U.K. cases, departmental enterprises were legally restructured as joint stock companies before their sale. Kelang Container Terminal was part of a larger port and was spun off as a new entity before its sale.

Similarly, labor force restructuring occurred in the British Airways and Aeromexico cases. Aeromexico was an example of extreme measures in labor restructuring: the government liquidated the firm and then allowed the new owners to rehire their own labor force.

Even though financial restructuring (e.g., adjusting debt to equity ratios) before selling a firm is a zero-sum game, or simply a wash, it might make the company appear more salable. In the case of Aeromexico, for instance, the government liquidated the company, sold the assets, and essentially carried the liabilities. Without this action, the government would have had to sell the company at a negative price, which is clearly politically unacceptable.

Another concern is how much to sell. There is a tendency to equate how much is sold with how much control is transferred, but that is not always the case. In the Telmex and Mexicana Airlines cases, for example, the government retained some shares but they are nonvoting. The advantage in such a mechanism is that it reduces the scope for government intervention while allowing the government to benefit if the shares appreciate in value. Such partial divestiture can have many of the advantages of a full divestiture—increased investment, as in the cases of British Telecom and Malaysia Airlines Systems, or management turnaround, as happened with Kelang Container Terminal. Partial divestiture also provides a way around the problem of limited absorptive capacity of capital markets when a large firm is sold. Selling in phases makes it possible for capital markets to handle the sale.

What mechanisms should be used in selling public enterprises? The simple answer is just about all of them. In most of the cases studied governments combined all sorts of mechanisms to sell a firm. For example, Chile used a reimbursable financial contribution mechanism, according to which consumers requiring new services received shares in return for paying in advance for these connections. These shares were then traded on the market to establish a market price. Later divestitures involved selling some shares to workers, sometimes at the stock market price, sometimes at a discount. And for some divestitures, such as Chile Telecom, shares were sold through public bids, with foreign participation welcomed.

The crucial point is to ensure sustainability. To begin with, it is important that buyers put in enough equity. In some of the early privatizations in Chile, buyers used one firm as collateral for others, a bad idea because as soon as there is a recession, firms go bankrupt and the government may have to take them over again.

Another general rule is to use public bidding procedures as much as possible to assure transparency and reduce political opposition. The highest bid is not necessarily the best one, however. Technical know-how may be an important consideration in sectors where the government wants to make sure that the buyers are able to run the company well.

As to who should actually be in charge of divestitures, there are two functions that need to be considered separately. Policymaking and decisionmaking ought to be centralized at the top, but execution is more efficiently handled at a lower level. Many countries have successfully followed that dual approach, Chile, Mexico, and the Philippines among them.

Whom to Sell to

The general principle is to sell to anyone who is willing to buy and has the money. Two special considerations may come into play in the case of foreign purchasers and employees. Foreign purchasers may bring access to fresh capital that may not otherwise be available, know-how, and motivation. And adding foreigners to the bidders' pool increases its size and makes it possible to get a higher price for the firm. On the negative side is the possibility of a leakage of benefits abroad and the general sensitivity to foreign ownership. The case studies show, however, that in most instances of foreign involvement the foreign owners benefited, but so did the national economy.

Workers constitute another special case. The advantages of selling to employees are obvious, the disadvantages less so. If shares are offered to workers at below-market prices, it could be argued that the employed are being favored over the unemployed. But the cases in Chile show that workers don't always have to be offered special prices to be enthusiastic participants. Shares were sold to workers at the stock market price in most cases. To avoid financing problems, workers were allowed to use their severance pay to buy shares.

When to Start

When it comes to the best time to start, some would say yesterday and some would say tomorrow, hoping that tomorrow never comes. We would say today, of course, provided that the recommended policies have been implemented.

11

THE JIGSAW PUZZLE

Nancy Birdsall

It is difficult to be one of the last speakers and still contribute any value added to what has been a brilliant set of papers and presentations. It seems to me that the researchers confronted a gigantic jigsaw puzzle and had to try to put it together without a picture of what it was supposed to look like. There were a lot of blue pieces, possible sky or ocean, and far fewer other-colored pieces that looked like parts of a boat or farmhouse. So very reasonably, as good jigsaw puzzlers would, the researchers took all the pieces with straight edges and set out the border. Then they moved on to the remaining parts of the puzzle that were the easiest to put together: the non-blue pieces. Soon, say down in the southeast corner of the puzzle, a boat or farmhouse began to emerge clearly.

I want to look for a moment at the pictures that have emerged from this set of research pieces and to consider them in terms of two sets of countries that were, for unavoidable reasons, left out of the study: the poor and institutionally bereft countries, most notably in Africa, and the economies in transition from socialist command economies to market economies, especially in Eastern Europe and the former Soviet Union. I would like to speculate about the likely benefits of divestiture in those economies and about what the research does or does not have to say about that. I will also briefly explore the difficulties of reaping the benefits of divestiture in those economies. Finally, I will consider the implications of these comments for the World Bank and policymakers, including many of you here.

Likely Benefits in Poor and Transition Economies

My very rough conclusion is that this research implicitly underestimates the potential benefits of divestiture in these other two sets of economies, at least in potentially competitive sectors. Essentially, it is the impossibility of doing this research, of measuring economywide benefits to divestiture, that accounts for the underestimation. I suspect that these economywide benefits would be enormous in these countries.

It seems evident that in well-run economies, with a dynamic private sector and a competent and honest government, public enterprises in competitive sectors are going to be reasonably well run—else those competent governments would already have handled the problems. But in a poorly run economy, where public enterprises are losing money, there are likely to be compounding distortions in many different markets. Not only is there a fiscal drain if the firms are losing money, but governments are likely to try to shore the firms up, exempting them from import duties, environmental regulations, and health and safety rules. Such favored treatment penalizes other parts of the private sector that are not exempted. Political pressures for higher wages and higher employment may result in segmentation of the labor market, fueling an upward spiral of higher wages and higher employment. And if the firms are producing inputs in a protected market, they are creating higher costs for industries that rely on those inputs for their production. So state enterprises may have huge negative effects economywide.

The researchers referred to these externalities as "atmospherics." In certain settings, I would argue, particularly in Africa, these negative atmospherics are so great that the benefits of divestiture would be substantial.

Difficulties Implementing Privatization

While the benefits are potentially enormous, so are the difficulties of reaping them in these types of economies. Just doing the privatization at all is likely to be a daunting task, let alone doing it right. I am not talking about the normative question of whether it should be done, but about whether it is likely to be done given the difficulties.

There are two ways to characterize these difficulties. First, there is a political problem because the gains are so diffuse. No interest group can know in advance that it will be certain to benefit from privatization, but the losers-to-be know who they are—the workers, the bureaucrats, and the managers involved in the public enterprises. So that's part of the privatization trap that Larry Summers mentioned.

The second difficulty is that in Africa and in the formerly socialist economies there may be no competitive private sector into which to privatize enterprises, and getting one established requires all kinds of institutional development first—contract enforcement, legal framework, a reasonable capital market. There is no simple answer. You can't just say "liberalize trade" and expect thereby to create competition. It would take quite a leap of imagination to believe that in many parts of Africa the grip of a noncompetitive private sector on certain kinds of productive activities could be unlocked simply by liberalizing trade.

The problems are compounded in the case of public enterprises with a natural monopoly. In the U.K. studies, the key to an effective regulatory body that won't get captured by special interests was found to be staffing it with people of unblemished reputation. For these other two sets of economies, that would seem to be the most difficult step: setting up that regulatory body.

A related issue is whether it takes more or less administrative capacity to regulate than to run an enterprise. Larry Summers wondered why we have a bias in favor of the status quo since it would seem to be just as hard to run as to regulate an enterprise. The bias in favor of the status quo is not only political, but technical and institutional as well. You can have a group of people with a good idea about how to run an aluminum enterprise, but not a clue about how to set up a regulatory agency. Nor does the legislature necessarily know how to establish the legal framework for the regulatory agency. So the bias is not only political, it is also institutional in settings where there is a tremendous scarcity of people with the necessary know-how.

Implications for the World Bank and Policymakers

In thinking about the privatization trap, it is important to recognize that there is a political and social equilibrium at the starting point in these settings. The research demonstrates, I think, that the fundamental problem with public enterprises is not internal inefficiency but their vulnerability to bad government behavior. That is shown by the fact that much of the gain from privatization, even in middle-income countries, comes from better pricing mechanisms, expansion, and increased investment and from locking in these benefits to prevent the government's return.

There is thus an equilibrium problem, which demonstrates that country conditions are central to the story. And this goes back to my jigsaw puzzle analogy. We have put together many of the pieces for middle- and high-income countries, but we still have this ocean of confusion about what the picture should look like for the rest of the world. If we think of the public enterprise problem in those settings as one symptom of government failure, that means that it will be difficult to fix that problem without fixing everything else.

My sense is that we have to look for opportunities to exploit shocks to this equilibrium. One type of shock is a shift in political power. Another is the mounting fiscal drain of public enterprises, which can eventually become so severe as to constitute a shock to the political and social equilibrium and force governments to rethink their position on public enterprises. Reducing donor support to public enterprises can also be thought of as a way to induce a change in the equilibrium. The critical issue is to recognize that one kind of change can be offset by another. Unless the political factors that created the equilibrium in the first place are changed, undesirable compensations are likely to creep in when efforts are made to change the public enterprises by privatizing them.

Research itself can play a role here. Information about the cost of this low-level equilibrium can be a powerful instrument for change. Research that clarifies the high cost, even in the narrow sense of the cost of keeping enterprises public when they might be privatized, can alter the equilibrium in some settings. I think particularly of countries in Africa and in certain parts of Latin America, where this kind of information could be a powerful tool—especially in countries that have open communications and relatively sophisticated policymakers and constituents who can understand the benefits, diffuse as they are, associated with privatization. Perhaps difficult to do in much of Africa, but less difficult in Eastern Europe and the former Soviet Union.

Several areas in which more work is needed emerge clearly from this study. Even after all the discussion about regulatory regime, we have yet to identify a minimum regulatory package for particular settings. That is certainly not the job of this research, but the research has crystallized the need for further work on the regulatory regime.

The study also suggests that much more work is warranted on partial divestiture and on leasing and certain forms of contracting out, even though they do not lock in the gains the way divestiture does.

We still have much to learn about distribution. I think we need to pay much more attention to concerns about the perception of fairness, to the envy part of the problem that Larry Summers referred to, as well as to the fairness part. Some of the suggestions that have come up about foreign participation are relevant here. Should foreigners be limited to a certain percentage share in divestitures? Do we have guidance on what that share should be? We tend to say, "Let foreigners in; it can only help." But given the tradeoffs, there may be limits to that, and we need to know where they are. How can we help governments avoid politically unacceptable concentration in a few hands as a result of divestiture or avoid problems with ethnic majorities or minorities? Divesting in stages, selling some shares now and some later, as prices go up, is another example of finding ways to privatize that will be politically acceptable.

Comments

David Newbery

Simple economic theory says the state should be able to run a business at least as well as the private sector. The state ought to be able to maximize profit by corporatizing, franchising, setting up management contracts, and the rest in exactly the same way as the private sector does. And when maximizing profits is not the appropriate thing to do, the state, unlike the private sector, can do something else. So the simple-minded view is that anything the private sector can do, the state can do better.

We also know that this is not the case. So what is wrong with our simple theory? I would suggest two things. One is that when producers are in the state sector, they have a comparative advantage in capturing the regulatory framework. In fact, the regulatory framework is usually so well captured when the enterprise is in the public sector that it is not even visible. That is not to say that those in the private sector are laggards when it comes to capturing regulatory mechanisms. But they are not quite as adept, and so it is a good move to transfer producers outside of this very cozy state sector.

The second argument is that governments find it difficult to commit to good future behavior. They find it particularly difficult, it would seem, to adequately reward success and punish failure. Investment is quintessentially a commitment to the future, and in the United Kingdom at least, managing an investment has always been problematic for the public sector. Thus the main benefit of transferring enterprises out of the public sector was not so much getting improved management or better pricing of output, but rather getting more investment done more sensibly. It is also very difficult to reward managers properly when they stay in the state sector. Civil servants by and large do not get paid very well, so there is a strong feeling that nobody else working in the public sector should be paid very well either. Thus for all sorts of good reasons, the government finds it difficult to do what is clearly sensible.

So in a fundamental sense what divestiture is all about is an attempt to change the political economy of power. It is an attempt to tilt the balance in a preferred direction and to entrench a more efficiency-oriented approach to managing the economy.

The problem with going into a country and telling the government that, say, the exchange rate is wrong, is that the authorities may change it, but there is no guarantee that they will not change it back again when you are not looking. And if you ask why things are the way they are in any country, the usual answer is that there is a balance of interest groups that likes it that way. You may be able to nudge the balance temporarily when the country is down and out and needs your money. But if that equilibrium of interest groups is the balance you tried to upset, it will most likely spring back again when you are no longer pushing against it. So if you want to make permanent changes, you have to change the balance of power. And that, I would argue, is a key element of a divestiture program.

Let us consider what the other benefits of divestiture are. If a government commits itself to a serious divestiture program, it has to think very carefully about how to make it successful, and that means dealing with many of these problems of commitment.

If the assets are fixed and have a low resale value, then obviously the resale value to the buyer depends on future profitability. And that will depend on such things as the freedom to set prices, the ability to raise and borrow money for investment, and the predictability of the future competitive and regulatory environment, particularly pricing policy. Most important is security of title to the profits. The buyer needs to be certain that the firm is not going to be renationalized when the next government comes into power.

The government has to face up to these concerns and reassure buyers that their expectations are realistic and will be met. Doing that requires establishing a regulatory system that works well and that is predictable and fair. And that means creating appropriate institutions—institutions that are needed in any case, but which the process of divestiture forces the government to recognize explicitly. Among these are a system of competition policy and a system of appeal and referral, to contest cases of arbitrary uses of power.

The U.S. system of regulating rate of return has been much criticized for encouraging overinvestment and goldplating. But it also solidly guarantees a fair rate of return, which reassures investors. Investors need to know that they will be able to enjoy the future returns to their investment, especially if the investment is expensive and durable. The RPI minus x formula is much less secure because the "x" gets renegotiated. How well the system works depends to a great extent on the trust that the regulated have in the process of regulation. So although there are enormous attractions in the RPI minus x formula from an incentives point of view, it is more demanding of the trust and confidence of the regulated.

A regulatory framework requires two steps. It has to be set up, which is fairly straightforward. And it has to instill confidence in its future operation, which is, of course, more difficult. It takes time to establish a reputation for performance, to demonstrate that the system actually delivers as promised.

Are there external mechanisms to accelerate that process? For instance, can the World Bank or the IMF help countries establish a reputation for consistent regulatory behavior? Would it, for instance, make sense to make access to funds conditional on that kind of behavior? It might in some cases, by raising the stakes and raising the costs of deviating from stated intentions.

In this framework it is interesting to look at the kinds of industries that are good candidates for privatization. Privatizing small enterprises is straightforward and can be done quickly. And airlines come up again and again in divestiture programs because the problem of commitment does not arise. No matter what the reputation of the government for honest dealing, it can usually sell an airline with no trouble.

Telecommunications is puzzling on the face of it because it is very capital intensive, and there is the risk that the buyer will need to put in a lot of money without earning a reasonable rate of return if domestic prices are held down to satisfy consumers. The question is whether the balance of power between the owner and the regulator or the government permits a satisfactory outcome. I would argue that the owners have very substantial power. If the regulatory environment fails to establish an acceptable framework for earning profits and operating commercially, the owner has the capacity to ruin the economy by shutting down telecommunications services. And that means that it is not very risky to let foreigners or anybody else run the company because they know that they have that power, and government has an easier job convincing potential buyers of its commitment to behave. So privatizing telecommunications and managing and regulating this very important and very visible industry allows a country to develop a reputation for having a good regulatory framework, thereby increasing its credibility in other activities.

The electricity industry is a rather interesting case. It shares with the telecommunications industry the threat of disaster for the country if things go wrong. It is not nearly so easy, however, for the owner to hold the country and the regulator for ransom because it is an easy matter to sack the entire electricity-generating management and hire another. It's been done.

Privatizing export-oriented industries like container ports seems to be very straightforward in the sense that objective standards of performance are easily derived from world market standards and prices. It is not particularly difficult to write contracts that permit deviations from those standards to be readily detected and that specify external mechanisms, say through the World Bank or the IMF, to be brought to bear.

On the question of how to get out of the privatization trap, the answer seems to be that if policy credibility has not yet been established, only a small part of the firm should be sold first. Then, when more confidence has been established, more shares can be sold at a higher price.

Looking at the commitment issue from the opposite end, I would argue that if a country is fortunate to have in place a government with a reputation for efficiency and honest dealing, there is a powerful argument for selling as fast as possible to lock in that commitment to efficiency.

There is one point on which I disagree with the conclusions of this study, and that is on the question of restructuring. And perhaps the disagreement is very small. The general argument here has been that the private sector is better at restructuring than the government. I would argue that when it comes to breaking up monopolies, that is patently untrue. The private sector has a very strong vested interest in preserving, creating, and generally trying to reassemble monopolies, and handing one over to the private sector is putting the fox in charge of the henhouse. So breaking up monopoly enterprises before privatization is absolutely central to trying to improve the competitive environment.

Panel Discussion

Heba Handoussa

In summing up my thoughts about this valuable study, I want to begin with some sobering reflections on the role of the state, which is being redefined in developing countries. For the least developed countries privatizing on any large scale is a luxury because of the scarcity of entrepreneurial skills and private savings and the great number of people living in poverty. That makes the state's role in saving and investment extremely important to a country's development.

It is relatively easy to find, as the studies have, that if we turn public enterprises into private firms, they will do well. But in a dynamic sense, can we be sure that the private sector will invest enough? Can we be sure that savings are adequate? It is a little like saying that foreign investors or managers can do a better job than domestic managers or investors. That does not mean that we want to turn the whole job over to foreigners.

The other result that we have not discussed sufficiently is that the study seems to show that management is not as important in turning companies around as theory would have it. More of the gains have come from investment growth and increases in labor productivity. That raises the question of how much gain can be achieved simply from reforming public enterprises without changing ownership. I think it would be useful to apply the study's methodology to this issue by looking at two five-year periods preceding privatization: the first five years, in which there was very little restructuring or liberalization going on in most developing countries, and the next five years, coinciding generally with the mid- to late-1980s, in which liberalization and reform were common, from getting prices right to getting rid of surplus labor. I think it quite likely that the gains from those reforms have been much larger than the gains from transferring ownership.

I have two suggestions for increasing the usefulness of this and other World Bank studies for policymakers in developing countries. One would be to distinguish more clearly between monopoly and competitive sectors, highlighting the relevance of regulation in the case of monopolies and of deregulation in the case of competitive sectors. Another would be to focus future studies on the role of the state, identifying the minimum degree of intervention needed in countries with widespread poverty and market failures.

Rolf Luders

Several people have stressed the advantages of separating ownership from control for realizing a better price for public enterprises. It seems to me that that runs into the problem of moral hazard and the likelihood that entrepreneurs will take advantage of the fact that they have control of a company for which they have put up very little capital and will use that advantage to extract large rents from the corporations. Chile's experience with selling firms on credit, by allowing purchasers to use one firm as collateral for another, is really very similar, as Ahmed Galal pointed out.

The discussion during these two days has been biased toward maximizing the price for the government. Leroy Jones did point out a few times that we should worry less about losses to the government and more about overall gains in welfare. But we seem always to have come back to the idea of maximizing the price for the government. The notion of separating ownership and control is related to that concern. But it seems to me that there are many circumstances, such as those in Chile in the 1970s and in Eastern Europe today, that do not warrant so much concern about maximizing price. For one thing, privatizing can bring an end to what has often been a net fiscal drain for the government of many decades' duration, and certainly governments will gain in that way.

I would like to consider briefly how the methodology developed for this study could help us make decisions about whether to privatize. I see the methodology as basically social project evaluation applied to divestiture. The project is privatization, the no-project case is keeping the enterprise public. As we all know, making this choice implies making marginal decisions. The structure of the economy is taken as given and privatization is assumed to be a marginal decision.

Now, this is a good methodology for countries like the United Kingdom, or even Chile in the 1980s, which have well-functioning market economies. In those cases the study results are very strong, and privatization is obviously welfare-improving.

However, for Chile in the 1970s and, I think, for many Eastern European and other countries today, the objectives are different. They are to transform a centralized economy into a working market economy. Privatization is thus not an objective in itself, but a condition for getting what we call a social market economy working. I think that in such cases the methodology could be very useful prospectively for selecting the method of privatization best suited to meeting a country's objectives. Obviously, the method of sale is going to influence the distribution of the welfare gains or losses between, for instance, foreigners and the domestic sector or between the government and the private sector. The method is also going to influence the effects on workers and on capital market development. For instance, Chile divested many more enterprises in the 1970s than in the 1980s, although their value in the two periods was about the same. The difference is that in the 1970s, privatization had very little effect on capital market development, whereas in the 1980s it had a tremendous effect. The same is true with savings. Privatization may improve saving, have no effect on it, or even have a negative effect on investment. Similarly with efficiency. The effect can be positive or negative depending on how the privatization is done.

The political regime can be important as well. I think that Chile probably could not have privatized in the 1970s without an authoritarian regime, because the whole environment was so different then. But privatization would not have happened even under a military regime had there not been a crisis as well. My impression is that conditions are so different in the world today that crisis alone would be enough in most countries to spark change.

Johannes Linn

Let me start by congratulating the researchers for an excellent, well-designed study. When I chair reviews of research proposals, I usually ask my colleagues five questions: Does the proposed study have a clearly articulated set of objectives? Do the objectives have policy and operational relevance? Is there a clearly articulated and defensible methodology? Is the study doable given the time and resources? And are the data available? I would say that this study would score very highly on all five questions and could yield many lessons about the well-designed research study.

There are three dimensions of the study that I find particularly interesting. One concerns its policy and operational relevance.

Certainly it helps that the study deals with a burning issue. But its relevance is greatly strengthened by its design. I agree with Rolf Luders that the way the methodology was implemented facilitates linking the findings with the political economy questions so crucial in turning the study into a useful tool for policy analysis.

The methodology is especially well-articulated for a set of case studies. The common methodology flows clearly and systematically through the case studies and accounts in large measure for its success.

We heard a lot of comments on specific findings, that they don't apply here or don't apply there. True. But I think that that is a hallmark of good research, that the questions are defined narrowly and the limitations stated clearly. I think that the summary paper very carefully delimited the applicability of the findings to the cases and contexts studied and did not claim that they applied more generally.

There is one sense in which the study's results could be said to be disappointing. They offer no clear and overwhelming conclusions that say "Do X" or "Do Y," "Don't do A" or "Don't do B." In fact, if you look at a summary of the primary sources of welfare changes in the case studies, you see how differentiated the results are. For most of the categories, I think you would find a greater number of *no effects* than of significant effects. And there seems to be very little pattern to the results—the effects are all over the place. So you have a situation with no strong, clear set of conclusions that you can take to your audience and say, "Here is what we found, here is what matters, this is the conclusion we draw."

The summary paper also cites some unexpected findings, one being that the productivity factors are not as significant as might have been anticipated. Actually, I come out on the other side on that issue—productivity improvement seems to me, from a review of the summary findings, to be the strongest effect. The summary sees the investment effect as being very strong. I don't. It is very strong in two or three cases, but overall it is not a very strong effect.

So I think the results need to be presented carefully. That is going to be difficult because I think the value of research lies not so much in drawing up strong results for clear policy messages—here they are, take them away and apply them—but in providing a framework for analysis. It is difficult to sell a framework when you are disseminating research findings.

Perhaps the single most disappointing aspect of the study is that it does not provide a clear, unequivocal answer to the question, "Does ownership matter?" In any case, it has not changed my mind on the topic. I came in with a fairly strong opinion about that issue. But I think that if you try to use the study to convince people who doubt it that ownership really matters, you may have trouble fully convincing them. I do not think that this is a sign of any weakness in the study. I think it is just the nature of the exercise you are engaged in.

In closing I would like to flag a few items that I call *missing issues*, a kind of wish list for future research. The most important one is what factors determine investment activity and investment financing after privatization? The study considered capital and financial markets primarily in terms of their importance to the sales process. We also need to know what kind of financing system will permit newly privatized companies to go on and do all the good things on the investment front that we want them to do.

Another missing element is an analysis of industrial organization. The study finds that efficiency gains are universally related to firm size. Does that mean it is worth breaking firms up wherever possible before sale? My hunch is that it might be, but I do not think that has been addressed.

A third issue—and this one surfaced from time to time in these discussions—concerns the sustainability of nonintervention, of a sound regulatory framework. In a different context, our colleagues have emphasized the nonsustainability of efficiency gains from public enterprise reform. Is there perhaps a similar problem in terms of nonintervention and maintaining sound policies and a sound regulatory framework in a context where the overall political economy in fact requires intervention and distortions?

Finally, what was the impact of the quality of management in these case studies? By that I mean, what was the effect of the management teams and management culture of the larger firms that took over the companies we have discussed?

Even without having this additional wish list, however, the study deserves commendation as an excellent example of good research.

INDEX

(Page numbers in italics indicate material in figures or tables.)